Authority, Legitimacy, and the *Qawm*: Historical Perspectives on Emergent Governance in Afghanistan

A Monograph
by
Major J. Keller Durkin
United States Army

School of Advanced Military Studies
United States Army Command and General Staff College
Fort Leavenworth, Kansas

AY 2008-2009

Abstract

AUTHORITY, LEGITIMACY, AND THE *QAWM*: HISTORICAL PERSPECTIVES ON EMERGENT GOVERNANCE IN AFGHANISTAN by Major J. Keller Durkin, U.S. Army, 46 pages.

The present situation in Afghanistan is not being resolved by the current U.S. strategic approach. Given the recent uptick in insurgent violence, the shift in emphasis with regards to Afghanistan, and the change in presidential administrations, the United States has arrived at a critical crossroads regarding its strategic approach to Afghanistan. The gravity of the situation warrants an in-depth look at the context of Afghanistan to properly frame the problem for decision makers and strategic planners. This monograph fills a portion of the gap in contextual knowledge on Afghanistan needed to inform that examination.

In order to focus the study, the monograph considers two evaluation criteria--ethnolinguistic groups and social structures--and two periods--the beginning of the Durrani Dynasty and the Great Game. It analyzes the historical emergence of central governance in Afghanistan and clarifies the propensity of the Afghan populace to respond to external authority and foreign intervention. This work references a myriad of sources from history, anthropology, and political science from 1816 to the present day to reach its conclusions.

The analysis highlights findings in two general areas. The first is Afghan identity. Afghanistan's diverse population is poorly characterized in the superficial and reductionist analysis that is predominately applied. In short, there is no "average" Afghan, despite the attempts to lump the population into neatly defined categories. Each Afghan identifies with one or more *qawms,* a social organization or identity group. The term is poorly understood, but essential in understanding the complex dynamics of interaction among the disparate Afghan communities. The second area is Afghan power structure. The current approach to establishing centralized governance in Afghanistan opposes the traditional power and authority mechanisms. The propensity of most of the *qawms* is to resist what they perceive as illegitimate authority. Historically, the only strong centralized governments that have succeeded in Afghanistan have done so by co-opting a sufficient number of the *qawms* and gaining access to external resources, ranging from the plunder of regional neighbors to direct aid from foreign governments.

The monograph recommends a continued in-depth analysis of the various facets of Afghan culture as well as two additional areas of study: the nature of U.S. interests in Afghanistan and a critical examination of the current manifestation of Afghan governance with respect to the expectations of the populace. It also recommends three actions to be taken by the U.S. government. The first is to change the scope of the planning horizon from the immediate future to the long term. The second is to reduce the signature of coalition forces, though this does not equate to reducing coalition efforts. The third is to make support to the Afghan regime conditional as opposed to absolute. This final change comes with the caveats of remaining engaged regardless of the level of direct assistance and not adopting an "all-or-nothing" approach to support.

TABLE OF CONTENTS

Introduction

The United States and the Fall of the Taliban

The United States began Operation Enduring Freedom (OEF) on October 7, 2001 in response to the al Qaeda attacks of September 11, 2001 and the subsequent refusal of the Taliban government to turn over Osama bin Laden. OEF's purpose was to capture Osama bin Laden, destroy al Qaeda, and remove the Taliban regime from power in Afghanistan.[1] On November 13, 2001 the United Islamic Front for the Salvation of Afghanistan, more commonly known as the Northern Alliance, seized the capital Kabul, assisted by United States and United Kingdom special operations forces and air support. By December 17, the al Qaeda stronghold in the Tora Bora Mountains had been seized. However, Osama bin Laden had managed to escape capture.[2]

As the Taliban rapidly capitulated, the United Nations convened a group of prominent Afghans in Bonn, Germany, to develop a plan to govern the country. This meeting produced the "Agreement on Provisional Arrangements in Afghanistan Pending the Re-Establishment of Permanent Government Institutions," more commonly known as the "Bonn Agreement."[3] The Bonn Agreement outlined the plan for the new Afghan government. It established an Interim Authority to coordinate an emergency *Loya Jirga* (Grand Council), creating the Transitional Authority. This new governing body would have eighteen months to establish a constitutional *Loya Jirga* to develop a new Afghan constitution. The writers of the Bonn Agreement selected Hamid Karzai to lead the Interim Authority. In June 2002, he was elected as President of the

---

[1]Stephen Tanner, *Afghanistan: A Military History from Alexander the Great to the Fall of the Taliban* (New York: De Capo Press, 2002), 292; GlobalSecurity.org, "Operation Enduring Freedom," http://www.globalsecurity.org/military/ops/enduring-freedom-plan.htm (accessed February 27, 2009).

[2]Tanner, 309.

[3]The Participants in the UN Talks on Afghanistan, "Agreement on Provisional Arrangements in Afghanistan Pending the Re-Establishment of Permanent Government Institutions," The United Nations, http://unama.unmissions.org/Portals/UNAMA/Documents/Bonn-agreement.pdf (accessed February 26, 2009).

Transition Government. Two years later, he was elected to a five-year term as the President of the Islamic Republic of Afghanistan in October 2004.[4]

The writers of the Bonn Agreement also requested the assistance of the United Nations to assist in the stabilization of the country. UN Security Council Resolution 1386 authorized the creation of the International Security Assistance Force (ISAF) to secure the capital of Kabul on December 20th, 2001.[5] The United States and a coalition of other countries continued to conduct combat operations under the auspices of OEF.

Progress Thus Far

Over seven years after the fall of the Taliban, Afghanistan is still in turmoil. President Karzai has declined in popularity, derisively called the "Mayor of Kabul" for his inability to effectively control much outside the city limits. A resurgent Taliban now operates in a large portion of Afghanistan, allied with a new organization--Tehrik-i-Taliban Pakistan, commonly referred to as the Pakistan Taliban--which is currently destabilizing Pakistan's government.[6]

ISAF assumed responsibility for security operations outside of Kabul in 2006, but has been unsuccessful at quelling the rising violence. The United States has begun to shift emphasis from a comparatively calmed Iraq and is now considering a "surge" of troops to Afghanistan to meet the rising threat and achieve stability. In the interim, U.S. air strikes, trying to compensate

---

[4]Ibid. The Constitution of Afghanistan of 1964 was used as a base document, with some provisions superseding it, such as those regarding the monarchy and some specific directives from the Bonn Agreement. Islamic Republic of Afghanistan--Office of the President, "A Brief Biography of President Hamid Karzai," http://www.president.gov.af/english/president_biography mspx (accessed February 27, 2009).

[5]United Nations Security Council, "Security Council Resolution 1386 (2001) on the Situation in Afghanistan," The United Nations, http://www.un.org/docs/scres/2001/sc2001 htm (accessed February 25, 2009).

[6]Simon Robinson, "Karzai's Kabul: Fit for a King?, *Newsweek,* April 18, 2002, http://www.time.com/time/world/article/0,8599,231457,00.html (accessed March 7, 2009). Afghan President Hamid Karzai has often been referred to as the "Mayor of Kabul" for his lack of power external to the city.

for low troop strength, have been increased dramatically. Though successful in killing insurgents, the U.S. has also been blamed for the increase in civilian casualties, both from collateral damage when striking legitimate targets and mistakes in targeting. Whether those killed were innocent civilians or indeed insurgents, the negative publicity surrounding them has decreased the support for the United States and ISAF.[7] In a 2008 survey conducted by the Asia Foundation, only 38 percent of those surveyed said Afghanistan was headed in the right direction. This was down from 64 percent in 2004. Additionally, those polled perceived the ineffectiveness of the government and corruption at all levels as major problems.[8]

Even with the lofty goals established by the Bonn Agreement accomplished and expanded assistance from the United States and the United Nations, the situation in Afghanistan appears to be deteriorating rapidly. The commander of ISAF, American General David McKiernan, recently stated in a press conference that U.S. and allied forces had been "stalemated" by the Taliban in southern Afghanistan. Though quickly adding that the insurgents could be defeated, he insisted that "we know we need additional means in Afghanistan, whether they are security or governance-related or socioeconomic-related."[9]

Methodology

With the shift in attention from Iraq to Afghanistan, the rising violence and resultant increase in U.S. forces deployed to the area, the U.S. strategy in Afghanistan is under review. In order to effectively develop a new strategy towards Afghanistan, it is imperative that the context

---

[7]*CNN*, "U.S., NATO Airstrikes Fuel Afghan Public Backlash," September 8, 2008, http://www.cnn.com/2008/WORLD/asiapcf/09/08/afghanistan.civilian.deaths report/index html (accessed March 7, 2009).

[8]The Asia Foundation, "Afghanistan in 2008: A Survey of the Afghan People," 5-7, 59. http://www.asiafoundation.org/country/afghanistan/2008-poll.php (accessed February 27, 2009).

[9]Lara Jakes, "US Commander: Troops 'Stalemated' in Afghanistan," *Associated Press,* http://hosted.ap.org/dynamic/stories/U/US_AFGHANISTAN?SITE=OHALL2&SECTION=HOME&TEMPLATE=DEFAULT (accessed February 27, 2009).

of the situation is understood by the strategy developers. This monograph explores the Afghan context to illuminate what strategy makers should be aware of as they proceed. It examines the history of the Afghan government. It looks at the multiple identities of the non-homogenous Afghan population, and attempts to pinpoint a critical path that success in Afghanistan must follow.

To further the development of an effective strategy, the context of the situation in Afghanistan must be closely examined. U.S. efforts to this point have rested on building and supporting a strong Afghan central government--something that Afghanistan has not had up to this point in its history. However, the author hypothesizes that improperly applied foreign support to a central Afghan government seeking to consolidate power is an invitation to failure and further conflict. This failure is by and large due to not understanding the role of or addressing the cultural subsets that compose Afghanistan's populace. The evidence points to two themes, the importance of disparate Afghan identities and the emergence of power structures. From this, the author proposes two recommendations for further study, an examination of core U.S. interests at stake in Afghanistan and an assessment of the current Afghan government's legitimacy through the eyes of its people, and to continue an intensive study of the range of disparate Afghan cultures. Additionally, the United States should adapt its approach in three areas to improve its strategic footing in Afghanistan: adjusting the planning horizon, reducing the signature of coalition military presence, and critically evaluating the level of support to the Afghan government. To support these conclusions, the monograph outlines critical aspects of Afghanistan.

Dr. Larry Goodson, a Professor of Middle East Studies at the U.S. Army War College and an authority on Afghanistan, outlined six factors for understanding the country in his 2001 book, *Afghanistan's Endless War*. Goodson uses these six factors--ethno-linguistic cleavages, social structures, religious ideology, the effects of recent conflict, geopolitical position, and limited economic development--to explain the context of Afghanistan and explain its state as of the time of publication, Afghanistan prior to September 11, 2001 and the fall of the Taliban.[10]

This monograph uses two of these factors--ethno-linguistic cleavages and social structures--as evaluation criteria to analyze the development of the Afghan state through history and the reaction of the populace toward it. For each criterion, the argument highlights the propensity of the populace to act. By understanding the context of Afghanistan along these criteria, the discourse serves as a guide to strategy development that will not run counter to the predisposition of the Afghan people. The monograph considers the development of Afghan governance in two eras--the emergence of the Durrani Dynasty and the Great Game--in terms of these evaluation criteria. It concludes with themes that reflect the plausibility of current and future efforts in Afghanistan along with specific strategy recommendations. However, before engaging in this, the monograph first considers the differing "prisms" regarding governance and the concept of propensity.

Two "Prisms" of Governance

The goals set by the authors of the Bonn Agreement to achieve a stable, functioning government were lofty, even before considering the complete dysfunction of Afghanistan's government systems wracked by more than two decades of war and the final insult of Taliban rule. Even by the efforts of the crafters of the Bonn Agreement, the leadership of the Islamic Republic of Afghanistan, and the support of the efforts of the U.S., the UN Assistance Mission to Afghanistan, and ISAF, Afghanistan's central government has failed to flourish. For those who propose to "fix" governance in Afghanistan, they must learn why Afghanistan's government has

---

[10]Larry P. Goodson, *Afghanistan's Endless War: State Failure, Regional Politics, and the Rise of the Taliban* (Seattle, WA: University of Washington Press, 2001), xiii-xiv. The other four factors that Goodson presents are also very important. However, they are not as central to the argument of the monograph and are therefore not discussed at length.

not developed efficacy and risks lapsing into failed state status; they must understand the nature of Afghanistan and its history with government. Before they consider this, they must examine their implicit assumptions about the nature of government itself. In "helping" Afghanistan, Western powers and non-governmental aid organizations have often failed to consider their bias-- the "prism" through which they view the role and function of government.

Western Conception of Government

One cannot equate government in Afghanistan to government in any Western country. Attempts to explain away difference, such as "it won't be Jeffersonian Democracy as we understand it," are but weak platitudes that fail to grasp the fundamental discrepancies between different systems of thought. Fred Riggs, a noted anthropologist who focused on Far East societies, described it as such:

> American theories of Public Administration are predicated on the assumption that public officials are always under the ultimate control of a political institution based on notions of popular sovereignty and the election of politicians able to reflect their interests and manage the bureaucratic organs of the state. My experience told me, however, that although copies of these Western political institutions might have been established in new states, they might well be so weak that they could not govern effectively.[11]

To explain the failure, Riggs developed the "prismatic model" where two different perspectives-- different cultures, or even different groups with different perspectives--could look at the same actions and interpret them as either good or bad based on the values of each respective culture. In essence, what one saw was based on the specific "prism" through which one looked at it.[12]

Foreign efforts aimed at aiding the building of Afghan governance have applied an uncritical Western view on the task at hand. Arguably two of the most influential framers of

---

[11]Fred Riggs, "Intellectual Odyssey: An Autobiographical Narrative First Draft," January 1999, http://www2 hawaii.edu/~fredr/autobio3.htm#3 (accessed February 20, 2009).

[12]Fred Riggs, *Thailand: the Modernization of a Bureaucratic Polity* (Honolulu: East-West Center Press, 1967), 375-376.

Western political thought are Thomas Hobbes and John Locke. The Westerners involved in rebuilding Afghanistan do not have to have cite their specific treatises covering natural law, sovereignty, the reason of the state (*raison d'état),* or anarchy; their conceptions of what government is supposed to be are culturally ingrained in them. These early theorists, as well as scores of others that followed them, have created the modern nation-builder's "prism" of what a government is or is not supposed to be, what is celebrated, and what is condemned. Even within similar countries (or for that matter within a single country), there are strongly held opinions implicit in the minds of these political theorists.[13]

While it is safe to assume that your average Afghan has not read Locke and Hobbes, simply handing out copies of political science textbooks is not a realistic solution to this incongruence. It is sheer folly to believe that one political narrative developed over a thousand years can be surgically replaced with another. At the time of Riggs's studies, the prevailing literature espoused the "escalator model . . . in which 'traditional' societies were expected to respond to the fresh breezes of 'modernity' by embracing changes that would, sooner or later, bring them into the new world of opportunity created, with our help, on the morrow of collapsed imperial control." Riggs's experiences in Korea, China, and Thailand led him to reject that approach as "traditions would not dissolve on an escalator taking a society from its old roots into the new age." It is also obtuse to dictate values from one society on another and assume that there will not be a reactionary response.[14]

While all societies evolve, and many societies experience social revolution, it is a dangerous prospect to attempt to dictate such change. In the case of Afghanistan, such efforts have a long history of abject failure.

---

[13]Lee Cameron McDonald, *Western Political Theory: From its Origins to the Present* (New York: Harcourt, Brace & World, 1968), 300-328.

[14]Riggs, *Intellectual Odyssey.*

Propensity and the Will of the Afghan People

In considering the way ahead for Afghanistan and its people, it is important to consider what the Afghan people will and will not find acceptable. If efforts to change the nature of governance in Afghanistan are contrary to the desires of the people, there will be resistance; if those efforts are anathema to the people, the confrontation will be more dramatic and the results even harder to achieve if possible at all.

In lieu of taking a Western conception of government and imposing it on an unwilling populace who views it as alien, a far easier and agreeable concept is to discern the propensity inherent in the situation--the essence of what the populace itself wants to have happen--and pursue that. In *A Treatise on Efficacy*, François Jullien outlines the Chinese approach of finding the propensity of the situation versus the Western approach of achieving goals. "[R]ather than depend on our tools, we should rely on the way that a process unfolds in order to attain the hoped-for result; rather than think of drawing up plans, we should learn to make the most of what is implied by the situation and whatever promise is held out by its evolution."[15] By examining the situation and determining what the targeted population would desire for itself, one would have removed the largest and most powerful obstacle to achieving that end. It may not be what western governments have envisioned for Afghanistan, but it is achievable. And if there is something that is both achievable and acceptable to the external Western governments who are working on building Afghan governance, then that is the most feasible solution. Outsiders must consider more than their own metaphorical prism in finding a solution; they must also consider the Afghan prism.

---

[15]François Jullien, *A Treatise on Efficacy: Between Western and Chinese Thinking,* trans. Janet Lloyd (Honolulu: University of Hawaii Press, 2004), 16-17.

Evaluation Criteria

A key element in understanding Afghanistan is recognizing the vast differences that exist within the Afghan population and the complex interaction these disparate identities bring. There are many aspects to consider: ethnicity, religion, linguistics, locale, profession wealth, recognition of government authority, and history. These factors help in determining each Afghan's *qawm*.[16]

The Social Structure of Identity – *Qawm*

The word *qawm* is derived from Arabic and it roughly translates to tribe or group. But this definition fails to encompass what the term means. *Qawm* is also a solidarity group of any conception; at the largest levels, it can equate to being part of an ethnic group or even a national identity. It can be a linguistic group, regardless of ethnicity, a tribe, a clan, a family lineage, or other description of kinship. It can be based on location, a village or region, or even a shared *watan* or "homeland." *Qawm* can even be based on occupation (for example military).[17]

One does not have a single, discrete *qawm*, but can be part of several. Which takes precedence is based on how strongly the individual identifies with one solidarity group versus another. Also, this identity is dynamic: primacy of *qawm* can be adapted to suit the needs of the

---

[16] *Qawm* can also be transliterated as *qaum, qowm,* or others. Unless it is presented in a direct quotation differently, *qawm* will be used as the spelling in this document. The proper plural form is *aqwam*, but "*qawms*" will be used in this document for clarity. The concept of *qawm* as presented here was derived from multiple sources, including: Barnett R. Rubin, *The Fragmentation of Afghanistan: State Formation and the Collapse of the International System* (New Haven, CT: Yale University Press, 1995), 20-25, 30, 41-45, 346; Olivier Roy, *Islam and Resistance in Afghanistan* (Cambridge, UK: Cambridge University Press, 1986), originally published in French as *L'Afghanistan: Islam et modernité politique,* (Paris: Éditions du Seuil, 1985), 10-29; Bernt Glatzer, "The Pashtun Tribal System," in *Concept of Tribal Society (Contemporary Society: Tribal Studies, Vol 5),* ed. G. Pfeffer and D.K. Behera (New Delhi: Concept Publishers, 2002), 265-282.

[17] Rubin, *The Fragmentation of Afghanistan*, 25-28.

group or the individual. Thomas Barfield described it succinctly when he described it as "a wonderfully flexible term . . . that indicates 'us' as opposed to 'them.'"[18]

More than a manner of self-identification, *qawm* is a system of loyalty. As an Afghan, your loyalty lies with the *qawm* you hold and your fellow *qawmis* (members of your *qawm*) as opposed to an external government system or rule of law. There is an ethnographic cliché that describes these loyalty ties: "It is me against my brothers; it is my brothers and me against our cousins; and it is our cousins, my brothers and me against the world."[19] When there is conflict, the loyalty is owed to the *qawm*. Within the *qawm*, customary law governs conduct. Between conflicting *qawms*, disputes can be put aside to deal with greater external threats shared by both-- a larger *qawm*. This explains the ability of the Afghan populace to overcome internecine struggles to defeat invaders. If it is in the *qawm's* best interest to band with another, it will do so. Of course, even during the height of the Soviet-Afghan War, *mujahidin* groups often fought each other as well as the Soviet and Democratic Republic of Afghanistan forces.[20]

Ethnic and Linguistic Groups

Afghanistan is made up of varied ethnic groups. The most numerous are the Pashtun, Tajik, Uzbek, and Hazara.[21] The Pashtun comprise the largest segment of the population of

---

[18]Thomas Barfield, "Afghan Customary Law and Its Relationship to Formal Judicial Institutions" (Monograph, United States Institute for Peace, 2003), 3. Professor Thomas Barfield is Professor of Anthropology at Boston University. Professor Barfield has conducted extensive research on Afghan and Central Asian culture. His current research focuses on war reconstruction and economic development in Afghanistan as well as its political reorganization.

[19]Thomas Barfield, "Problems in Establishing Legitimacy in Afghanistan," *Iranian Studies,* 37, no. 2 (June 2004): 263-293, 266. Barfield and Glatzer both identify that *qawms* tend to be stronger at the local level. It is often the case that Tajiks and Pashtuns that are located would form a stronger *qawm* based on shared locale then a more abstract Pashtun loyalty.

[20]Tanner, 259, 272.

[21]There are numerous other, smaller ethnolinguistic groups in Afghanistan including the Aimaq, Turkomen, Farsiwan, Qizilbash, Kirghiz, Baluch, Bruhai, Nuristani, Sikh, and Hindu. Many of the groups are sometimes rolled up with others based on shared commonalities. For further information on the

Afghanistan, with roughly about 40 to 45 percent of populace, roughly 12.8 million people. The word "Afghan" is the Farsi word for Pashtun. In essence, Afghanistan literally means "The Land of the Pashtuns." The Pashtun claim to be the largest tribal society in the world. The majority of the Pashtun population, however, lives in Pakistan, making up approximately 15 percent of that country's population, 23.8 million people, and double that of the Afghan Pashtun population. This separation plays a major role in the tumultuous relationship between Afghanistan and Pakistan over the issue of "Pashtunistan"--an imagined national homeland for the Pashtun ethnic group.[22]

The Pashtun are split into two major tribal confederations--the Durrani and the Ghilzai-- with an assortment of tribes, sub-tribes or clans, and lineage lines therein. The Pashtun claim common heritage and organize along lines of agnatic (paternal) familial descent. The significance of tribal heritage and culture varies among the Pashtun depending on a number of factors. In order to claim Pashtun heritage, one must be ethnically Pashtun, speak the Pashtu language, and follow the code of *Pashtunwali*, or "doing Pashtun." The code is customary law amongst the Pashtun and, as such, has variable interpretation. How strictly a Pashtun abides by the code of *Pashtunwali* will be explored in the subsection that explores the categories of *qalang* and *nang*.[23]

---

characteristics of some of these groups, see Louis Dupree, *Afghanistan* (Princeton, NJ: Princeton University Press, 1973), 59-64.

[22]Population numbers for all ethnic groups was derived from: The CIA World Factbook, "Afghanistan," The Central Intelligence Agency, https://www.cia.gov/library/publications/the-world-factbook/geos/af html (accessed February 28, 2009). The exact breakdown of ethnic groups is not accurately known due to the lack of an official, accurate census. There is a wide discrepancy in numbers claimed by different agencies. Population data for Pakistan: The CIA World Factbook, "Pakistan," The Central Intelligence Agency, https://www.cia.gov/library/publications/the-world-factbook/geos/pk html (accessed February 28, 2009). The claim to the largest tribal society was included in, and qualified as unverified, in Glatzer, "The Pashtun Tribal System," 265-282, 3. There are multiple sources which attribute the word "Afghan" to be the Farsi word for "Pashtun," though there is debate as to the original etymology of the word.

[23]Louis Dupree, *Afghanistan*, (Princeton, NJ: Princeton University Press, 1973), 184-185; Barfield, "Afghan Customary Law and its Relationship to Formal Judicial Institutions," 4-5. Dupree's chart on pp 184-185 shows the best description yet of the hierarchy of Pashtun and other ethnic groups. As

The Durrani Pashtuns ruled Afghanistan almost exclusively from the rise of Ahmad Shah Durrani in 1747 to the 1978 coup which toppled President Mohammad Daoud. Also notable is the fact that current President of Afghanistan, Hamid Karzai, is also a Durrani Pashtun. The Pashtuns consider themselves to be the rightful rulers of Afghanistan.[24]

The second largest ethnic group in Afghanistan is the Tajik, comprising approximately 30 percent of the population. The Tajik are non-tribal, primarily drawing their *qawm* from their area of origin. Despite the lack of tribal organization, they follow lineage to a certain degree. They primarily speak Dari, the Afghan version of Farsi. Tajiks are located primarily in the north and northeast part of the country and form a large portion of the population of Kabul. Looking at the Tajik reveals one of the problems with subdividing Afghanistan into discrete ethnic groups. Tajiks, as outsiders categorize them, do not recognize themselves as such. The base of the primarily "Tajik" Northern Alliance would identify themselves as Panjshiri, after the Panjshir Valley where they came from. "Tajiks" in Kabul would see themselves as Kabulis. It would be specious to group Tajiks as an ethnic whole, because they do not strongly identify themselves as such.[25]

Dupree notes, "the terms used are fuzzy because it is difficult to generalize for all groups, or even within specific groups." Barfield outlines the conception of being Pashtun.

[24]M. Hassan Kakar, *Afghanistan: The Soviet Invasion and the Afghan Response, 1979-1982* (Berkeley: University of California Press, 1995), 1,4,15. There were numerous changes in lineage; the line was not uninterrupted. An ethnic Tajik, Habibullah, did seize power in 1923 and rule for nine months. This breakage in line did have a negative impact on Tajik-Pashtun relations at the time. Regarding Hamid Karzai's tribal lineage, Abdulkader Sinno, "Explaining the Taliban's Ability to Mobilize the Pashtuns," in *The Taliban and the Crisis of Afghanistan,* ed. Robert D. Crews and Amin Tarzi (Cambridge, MA: Harvard University Press) 2008, 59-89, 83. Regarding Pashtun sense of authority, Robert D. Crews and Amin Tarzi, ed., *The Taliban and the Crisis of Afghanistan* (Cambridge, MA: Harvard University Press, 2008), 24. "Many Pashtuns have entertained the idea that Afghanistan is their land, where non-Pashtuns may live but do not fully belong."

[25]Rubin, *The Fragmentation of Afghanistan,* 30. From Rubin's notes, an alternate definition of Tajik, separate from ethnicity, was "anyone integrated into urban, Persian-speaking culture, including some of Uzbek descent."

Both Pashtu and Dari are Indo-Aryan languages and the *lingua francas* of Afghanistan, which elevates the importance of these two ethnic groups above the others. The fact that a large proportion of the population is bilingual helps lessen barriers between the Tajiks and Pashtuns. Outside of the traditional tribal areas of the Pashtun Belt, there has been a great comingling between ethnic groups through intermarriage and linguistic penetration. This is even more the case in very urbanized areas. As a result, the ethnic distinctions tend to matter less now than in the past. Afghans of all ethnic groups are likely to look locally for their *qawm*.[26]

The Uzbeks make up about 10 percent of Afghanistan's population. They are of Turkic origin and speak Uzbeki, a Turkic-Mongolian language. They are a tribally organized society, though the significance of the tribal structure varies and the tribal aspect of their culture is generally not as strong as the prevalent Pashtun tribal culture. They are primarily located in the northern portion of Afghanistan along the border of present day Uzbekistan.[27]

The Turko-Mongol Hazaras form approximately the same percentage of the population as the Uzbeks. They predominately speak Dari. The Hazara are believed to be the descendents of Genghis Khan's forces and are recognizable by their very pronounced Asiatic features. The Hazara inhabit the mountains in the center of Afghanistan in an area referred to as the Hazarajat. One very important note about the Hazara: they are the bulk of the Shi'a population of Afghanistan. The rest of the population of Afghanistan is almost exclusively Sunni Muslim. The Hazara have experienced extensive and violent discrimination at the hands of the other ethnic groups of Afghanistan, most often from the Pashtun. A large portion of this is due to their

---

[26]M. Hassan Kakar, *Afghanistan*, 1.

[27]Rubin, *The Fragmentation of Afghanistan*, 26.

adherence to the Shi'ite faith. The Hazara are closely aligned with their Shi'a coreligionists and fellow Dari/Farsi speakers in Iran.[28]

As Afghanistan's borders were formed by the machinations of external powers, the country was not formed around a homogenous group, but around this eclectic collection of ethnicities. While the boundaries on a map may appear to be clear to the outsider looking in, they are less so to the individual on the ground where they may not mean anything or even be known. Even in a more detailed map that outlines predominately ethnic areas, there is an incongruence between clean lines drawn by cartographers and anthropologists, the perceptions of the disparate communities, and the dynamic interactions of ethnic groups. In fairly static and non-stressful circumstances, this diversity can be an innocuous means of self-identification. However, in times of conflict or under pressure, ethnicity is a channel for violent reaction, such as the continued exploitation of the Hazara and the brutalization of the Pashtun in the north after the fall of the Taliban.[29] At other times, ethnicity has been used as a tool to leverage power, such as Amir Abdur Rahman's "Afghanisation" policy of the 1880s and 1890s, where rival co-ethnic groups were fragmented and rival ethnic power bases disrupted through forced migration.[30] Regarding the role of ethnicity in Afghanistan, it is also critical to note that when the Bonn Agreement was

---

[28]Dupree, *Afghanistan,* 60. Regarding atrocities against the Hazara by the Taliban: Crews and Tarzi, ed., *The Taliban and the Crisis of Afghanistan,* 31. The Hazara have been discriminated against and brutalized through long stretches of Afghanistan's history. Abdur Rahman Khan was notably brutal in suppressing the Hazara in the 1880s.

[29]Human Rights Watch, "Paying for the Taliban's Crimes: Abuses Against Ethnic Pashtuns in Northern Afghanistan," *Human Rights Watch* 14, no. 2 (April 2002), 1-2. http://www.hrw.org/legacy/reports/2002/afghan2/afghan0402.pdf (accessed April 19, 2009).

[30]Amin Saikal, *Modern Afghanistan: A History of Struggle and Survival* (London: I.B. Tauris, and Co, 2004), 38-9; Christian Bleuer, "'Afghanisation:' A Rather Unfortunate Neologism," The Ghosts of Alexander: The Afghan Campaign, 2001 to Whenever, entry posted February 11, 2009, http://easterncampaign.wordpress.com/2009/02/11/afghanisation-a-rather-unfortunate-neologism/ (accessed April 19, 2009). Of note, Christian Bleuer is a PhD candidate whose "academic work focuses on rural and peripheral social, political and military dynamics in Afghanistan and Southern Central Asia." He runs the "Ghosts of Alexander" weblog and is the creator/editor of The Afghanistan Analyst, an online research portal for Afghanistan, available at http://afghanistan-analyst.org/default.aspx.

being crafted, there was no effort by the competing factions to split the country along ethnic lines--a "Balkanization" if you will. All parties recognized the value of the unique identity of Afghanistan in the international community and accepted the idea of Afghanistan as a multi-ethnic state. In examining this phenomenon, Thomas Barfield points out the importance of the various *qawms* in determining loyalty along ethnic or other lines, and that the legitimacy of other ethnic groups was not in question but the matter of authority was.[31] Given the varied role and impact of ethnicity explored herein, the question remains how to consider ethnicity. Rather than formulating conclusive statements on ethnicity and its role in Afghanistan's system of governance, it is more important to explore the dynamics of ethnicity and how the varying ethnic groups interact. Incumbent in this is the understanding that one cannot develop a universal set of norms for dealing with each ethnic group.

Pashtunwali

As mentioned before, to be considered a Pashtun, a person must be of Pashtun ethnic descent, speak Pashtu, and adhere to the code of *Pashtunwali*, literally translated as "doing Pashtun." The *Pashtunwali* code is arguably the most important guiding force of the life style and ethical code of the Pashtun people, especially those that find themselves outside of central government control. *Pashtunwali* is both a personal code of ethics and a code of customary law. It is important to recognize that not every Pashtun tribe or individual sees these tenets equally nor practices them uniformly. As it is customary law and not codified, it has evolved differently with the many *qawms* of the Pashtun. Mountstuart Elphinstone, the British explorer and diplomat who was among the first Westerners to study the Pashtun, observed this variability first hand.

---

[31]Thomas Barfield, "Afghanistan is Not the Balkans: Ethnicity and its Political Consequences from a Central Asian Perspective." *Central Eurasian Studies Review* 4, no. 1 (Winter 2005): 1-8, http://www.cesr-cess.org/pdf/CESR_04_1.pdf (accessed February 20, 2009).

> The system of government which I have described, is so often deranged . . . that it is seldom found in full force; and must, therefore, be considered rather as the model on which all governments of tribes are formed than a correct description of any one of them. There is probably no case where some link is not wanting the chain of authorities, which ought to descend from the Khaun to the heads of families. . . . The whole constitution is also sometimes overturned. . . . frequently, the chiefs are neglected; and every subdivision, every quarter, and even every family, throws of its dependence on its superiors,and acts according to its own interest and inclination.[32]

Elphinstone's message from 1815 rings true today. As a system of law or a political system, *Pashtunwali* is not written in concrete, nor is it universally applied. However, there are some more or less universally accepted tenets: *badal* or revenge, *melmastia* or hospitality, and *nanawati* or asylum for those that seek it.[33]

The "blood revenge" concept of *badal* is probably the most well-known of the tenets of *Pashtunwali*. If a Pashtun has been wronged, it is essential to the maintenance of his personal honor and the honor of his *qawm* to redress that wrong. There is no time limit to this settling of scores. This timelessness is well illustrated in the tale of the Pashtun who waited one hundred years to take revenge and chastised himself for acting too soon. The phrase "revenge is a dish best eaten cold" is also believed to be Pashtun in origin.[34] If the offender is not available, then any of his male relatives will serve in lieu. If the offended does not seek *badal* then it is the requirement of his male relatives to seek vengeance. The requirement to seek revenge serves both as an arrestor and a catalyst of conflict. It serves as the enforcement mechanism of *Pashtunwali*. The

---

[32]Mountstuart Elphinstone, *An Account of the Kingdom of Caubul: And Its Dependencies in Persia, Tartary, and India* (1815; repr., Whitefish, MT: Kessinger Publishing, 2008), 162.

[33]See Barfield, "Afghan Customary Law and its Relationship to Formal Judicial Institutions," Glatzer, "The Pashtun Tribal System." Every book on Afghanistan has a section on *Pashtunwali*. Anthropologists Glatzer and Barfield provide the most thorough examination there of. There are many conflicting definition of the various tenets, likely owing to the various interpretations. However, *badal* (revenge), *melmastia* (hospitality), and *nanawati* (asylum) are agreed upon, though there are differing transliterations. Of note, Glatzer states that Pashtuns in the western reaches of Afghanistan would not refer to this sytem as *Pashtunwali*, but *rawaj*, though the content is essentially the same.

[34]Barfield, "Afghan Customary Law and its Relationship to Formal Judicial Institutions," 8.

clear understanding that violations of the code against another will be met with severe and unavoidable retribution serves as a deterrent for actions in violation of the code. But, once invoked, *badal* can become a self-perpetuating cycle of violence as opposing sides are obligated to seek retribution in turn.[35]

There is a popular misconception that fulfilling *badal* must always be accomplished by blood, though this is not true. There are multiple ways to redress wrongs other than through violence. One of the functions of the *jirga* or tribal council is to provide a forum where injuries to honor can be assuaged without bloodshed. The decisions of the *jirga* bind those parties to arbitration and will result in a payment of some sort (not strictly monetary) to satisfy the aggrieved party. Additionally, temporary truces can be settled between warring factions if an external threat requires it. During the Soviet-Afghan War, many truces were agreed upon to allow an unfettered focus on the threat of the Soviets and Marxist factions of Afghans that served as a greater threat.[36]

Melmastia is the tenet of hospitality and outlines the rights and obligations of Pashtuns toward guests. Guests are accepted without reservation, given the best of what the host has to offer, and provided absolute protection. The host becomes personally liable for the safety of his guest and is honor-bound to safeguard him. In exchange, the guest limits his stay, does not purposefully bring trouble for his host, and accepts his host's authority. *Melmastia* even supersedes *badal*. Strict adherence brings great honor; violation brings tremendous dishonor.[37]

---

[35]Ibid, 5-8.

[36]Christian Bleuer, "Pashtuns Must Have Their Revenge! Sometimes!," The Ghosts of Alexander: The Afghan Campaign, 2001 to Whenever, entry posted June 27, 2007, http://easterncampaign. wordpress.com/2007/06/27/pashtuns-must-have-their-revenge-sometimes/ (accessed February 27, 2009). For a thorough description of arbitration procedures, see Barfield, "Afghan Customary Law and its Relationship to Formal Judicial Institutions,"

[37]Barfield, "Afghan Customary Law and its Relationship to Formal Judicial Institutions," 7.

Closely related is the concept of *nanawati* or sanctuary. Barfield describes it as the "right to seek protection, request pardon or demand help from a more powerful person or kin group by a weaker one. In its best known form, someone leaves his own community looking for permanent protection."[38] Louis Dupree illustrates the concept best with a Baluch morality tale:

> The tents had been pitched and the women prepared the evening meal. As dusk approached, so did a rider out of the desert. He rode to the tent of the Khan and threw himself from his horse, prostrated himself at the Khan's feet, and demanded protection. He was being followed, he claimed, by a large band of horsemen with whom his family had a blood feud. The old Khan, wise beyond years, and pure as his white beard, granted the supplicant asylum. The man was led to the guest tent and there fed, and told to prepare himself for the evening.
>
> The Khan's young son came to his father and cried, "Oh my father! That is Badshah Gul, who but two months ago slew my brother and your son."
>
> "Yes, my son, but now he is a guest in our camp and he asked for asylum. We have given him asylum. And remember my son, even if it takes a hundred years, your brother's death, my son's death, will be avenged."
>
> The young son, inflamed, left his father's tent and, taking his brother's dagger from its honored place, crept to the guest tent and buried the dagger into the breast of the guest, as they had buried his brother two months before.
>
> The next morning, amid cries and lamentations, the body of the guest was discovered. Tearing his clothing, ripping his turban in agony, the old Khan cried, "Who could have done this? Who could have brought dishonor on the name of our family? The camps of the Baluch will forever condemn us for this dishonor!"
>
> The young son threw himself at his father's feet and begged forgiveness, saying that in a moment of blind rage, he had dishonored the group.
>
> The old Khan took the knife which had killed the guest and plunged it into the heart of his son.[39]

The personal honor of the Pashtun, or *ghayrat*, is the compelling force of *Pashtunwali*. While most disputes under the code are centered on "*zar, zan,* and *zamin*" (gold, women, and land), the most important thing to defend is *nawus*, the honor of women. *Pashtunwali* is customary law and

---

[38]Ibid, 8.

[39]Dupree, 127-128. Though not Pashtun, the Baluch adhere to an ethical code and customary law similar to *Pashtunwali*.

differs from other forms of law, such as state law or Islamic *sharia* law. Each of these three systems represents different forms of legitimacy, with endemic conflicts with the others.[40] How *Pashtunwali* relates to these competing forms of legitimacy depends on if that Pashtun community is *qalang* or *nang*.

The Division of the Pashtun – *Qalang* and *Nang*

The characterizations *nang* and *qalang* define the dichotomy of Pashtun affiliation. Pashtuns recognize different levels of external authority or government control. The area of relative government authority is known as the *hukumat*; beyond the *hukumat* are the lands where the tribes are self-governing--*yaghistan* or the "land of rebels." The *qalang* Pashtuns who live in the *hukumat* recognize the authority of hierarchical structures and maintain patron-client relationships with reified positions of authority. They pay taxes and rent (as well as collect them). The patronage systems are enduring and formal, such as the *jagirdari* system that prevailed under Pashtun ruler Ahmad Shah Durrani.[41]

The *nang* Pashtuns, however, maintain their independence from centralized government control. They reject patron-client relationships. Among the *nang* tribes, adherence to *Pashtunwali* is not just a defining factor of Pashtun identity but the absolute law of the land. Truly egalitarian, there is no recognized compelling hierarchy beyond the *jirga* of the *qawm*. The leadership of the tribe is based on the consensus of the *jirga* and is very dynamic in nature. Barnett Rubin uses a Pashtun proverb to illustrate the dichotomy: "Honor (*nang*) ate up the mountains; taxes (*qalang*) ate up the plains."[42]

---

[40]Barfield, "Afghan Customary Law and its Relationship to Formal Judicial Institutions," 5-8, 14, 44.

[41]Rubin, *The Fragmentation of Afghanistan,* 28.

[42]Rubin, *The Fragmentation of Afghanistan,* 28; Dupree, 104. In *nang* areas, there is sometimes a conflict between Islamic *sharia* law and pre-Islamic *Pashtunwali*. Because of the isolated nature of these

As is the case with conceptions of *qawm*, there is a dynamic aspect to the concepts of *qalang* and *nang*. There is not a strict divide, but varies in degrees. Elphinstone noted "On the whole, it is generally observable that the tribes most under the King's influence are most obedient to their Khaun, though there are some striking exceptions to the rule."[43] The causality of this is not clear, but it can be argued that the reverse is also true, that an authority figure's ability to exert control over the tribe determines it obedience: without the power, there would be no obedience. The *qalang* are such because the central authority has the means to enforce it. As such, the degree of autonomy varies through time based on the ability of hierarchical organizations to assert control over the *qawms*. It would be a mistake to assume that a *qalang* Pashtun *qawm* has lower standards of honor, just a different interpretation. Also, it would be incorrect to equate Pashtuns in urban areas who have been effectively detribalized with those in a semi-urban area who still adhere to *Pashtunwali*. One noticeable trait of the *qalang* is their ability to organize based on their acceptance of external authority structures as compared to the acephalous *nang*. But it would be incorrect to assume that just because someone declares himself an authority that *qalang qawms* would supplicate themselves. On the other hand, *nang qawms*, though lacking in organizational capabilities due to their dynamic and volatile authority structures, are even more unlikely to accept the direction of external actors.[44]

---

groups, they do not recognize the differences, per se, but tend to follow *Pashtunwali* and equate it with *sharia*. With the rise of the Taliban, this led to additional conflict between *Pashtunwali* and *sharia*. See also Ahmed Rashid, *Taliban: Militant Islam, Oil, and Fundamentalism in Central Asia* (New Haven, CT: Yale University Press, 2000), 89-90.

[43]Elphinstone, *An Account of the Kingdom of Caubul,* 163. Glatzer also references this quote in "The Pashtun Tribal System," 11.

[44]Palwasha Kakar, "Tribal Law of Pashtunwali and Women's Legislative Authority," http://www.law.harvard.edu/programs/ilsp/research/kakar.pdf (accessed September 7, 2008); and Barfield, "Problems in Establishing Legitimacy in Afghanistan," 263-293. 13th Century Muslim historian Ibn Khaldun goes into great detail regarding the concepts behind qalang and nang groups, though not using those terms. See Abd Ar Rahman bin Muhammad ibn Khaldun, *The Muqaddimah*, 1377, trans. by Franz Rosenthal (repr., Princeton, NJ: Princeton University Press, 1989), http://www.muslimphilosophy.com/ik/Muqaddimah/ (accessed January 8, 2009).

A Point of Caution

These categories have been presented in an attempt to classify the diversity among the various components of the Afghan population. It is important for the reader to understand that these lines are not clear. It would be reductionist and disingenuous to attempt to predict behavior on externally defined and broad-based demographic categories alone. For example, *Pashtunwali* is a central theme in Pashtun life, but it is a form of customary law that is not universally defined or practiced. While two groups may rigidly apply *Pashtunwali*, they can be vastly different in practice given their unique interpretations. Assuming that a Pashtun will react in accordance with an abstract, universal interpretation of *Pashtunwali* like it was preprogrammed code is ludicrous. The context of the *qawm* must be considered at the very least, and the individual will always retain a degree of personal autonomy. In presenting this primer on *qawm* and ethnicity, the monograph illustrates on a broad scale the complexity of Afghan social groups, but cannot describe any specific one given the richness and specificity that such a description would require. Also, the reaction of dissimilar Afghan *qawms* to one another cannot be directly applied to one of those *qawms* and its reaction to an even more foreign Western force.[45]

Governance in Afghanistan: Two Case Studies

The history of governance in Afghanistan is far too nuanced and complex a topic to cover adequately in this monograph. To apply the evaluation criteria on emergent Afghan governance institutions, this monograph presents two case studies. The first examines the rise of the Pashtuns under Ahmad Shah Durrani as an example of internally developed governance in Afghanistan. The second case study considers "The Great Game"--the competition between imperialist ambitions of Czarist Russia and Britain in the 19th century. It shows the emergence of

---

[45]Christian Bleuer, "The Afghan Individual as a Unit of Analysis," The Ghosts of Alexander: The Afghan Campaign, 2001 to Whenever, entry posted April 7, 2008, http://easterncampaign.wordpress.com/ 2008/04/07/the-afghan-individual-as-a-unit-of-analysis/ (accessed February 20, 2009).

governance within the country when faced with external pressures. It is particularly illustrative because it shows historical Afghan reaction to both direct intervention and an indirect approach. Both case studies illuminate the role of *qawms* and ethno-linguistic groups with respect to the central authority.

Ahmad Shah Durrani and the Beginning of Pashtun Hegemony

Ahmad Shah Durrani established a Pashtun confederation in 1747 which evolved into the first durable, supra-tribal Afghan government.[46] After gaining an initial mandate from his native tribe, Durrani expanded his power base to a larger segment of the various Pashtun tribes and conquered large swaths of non-Pashtun areas. He used a combination of coercion and appeasement to secure the loyalty of other Pashtuns. He established a balance of power by isolating potential rivals and dealing with them at a local level. He established government systems outside of tribal control. Probably most critical to his success was recognizing the limits of his power and not overextending himself.

Prior to Durrani's rise, power was granted by the consensus of the tribal councils or *jirgas*. With the wealth he acquired through service under Nadir Shah, Durrani was able to temporarily secure the loyalty of various other Pashtun tribes. With this composite army of tribes,

---

[46]See Dupree, *Afghanistan*, and Elphinstone, *An Account of the Kingdom of Caubul*. The rise of Ahmad Shah Durrani is a sea change in Afghan governance. Prior to Durrani's rise to power, what is now Afghanistan was the domain of the Safavid Persian Empire. Abdali Pashtuns, the forbearers of the Durrani line, had joined the Safavid leader, Nadir Shah, to fight fellow Pashtuns as well as the Mughal Empire. In 1747, Nadir Shah was murdered by assassins, but Ahmad Khan Abdali his Pashtun cavalry commander was able to escape, along with a large chunk of Shah's wealth, including the famous Koh-I-Noor ("Mountain of Light") diamond. Ahmad Khan found himself in a position of enormous opportunity. For the moment, the influence of the Safavid Persians, the Mughals of India, and the Uzbeks of the north are all at a low point. The Abdali Pashtuns selected Ahmad Khan as their leader and he renamed himself Ahmad Shah Durrani. Part of the significance of this name change was that Shah was a higher title than Khan. Durrani was adapted from Durr-I Durran, meaning "Pearl of Pearls," and reflected his trademark pearl earring. The Abdali tribe was henceforth known as the Durrani (though this point is debated by some scholars). He was not, as some claim, made King of Afghanistan at this point--there was no such position at the time. However, his unique experiences, wealth, and charisma allowed him to follow a divergent path away from a traditional Pashtun leadership role.

he was able to lead expeditions that conquered large swaths of non-Pashtun areas, both to the Tajik north and, more important, to the rich areas on the western edge of the Mughal Empire. These conquests provided him with the capital that he needed to maintain his control over the allied tribes.

But the loyalty of the *lashkars* or tribal armies that enabled these conquests was first to their *sardars* or tribal commanders, not Ahmad Shah Durrani. To solidify and stabilize this support, Durrani used *jagirdari,* a quasi-feudal system of land ownership, to both reward supportive tribal leaders and make their continued wealth and success dependent on him. *Jagirs*, or large tracts of land, were distributed to tribal leaders, *jagirdars*, in exchange for their pledged support. Those Pashtun tribes that were closer to Durrani were rewarded best and asked to contribute the least. So long as Durrani had enough *jagirdars* supporting him, he could suppress those that strayed.[47]

But the even so, the Afghan state was far from universally accepted. Elphinstone notes how closely the monarch kept his kinfolk, the Durrani tribe, under his authority, while elevating them over the other tribes of the Pashtun to placate them to some degree. Far from instilling a universal sense of Pashtun nationalism, the tribes "had ever regarded him as a powerful enemy, rather than a magistrate by whom they were protected, and to whom they owed loyalty and attachment." For the egalitarian Pashtun, the idea of subjugation by a fellow kinsman raised "even more jealousy than the tyranny of a foreign master."[48]

---

[47]T. A. Heathcote, *The Afghan Wars: 1839-1919* (Staplehurst, Kent, UK: Spellmount Limited, 2003), 9-10; Vartan Grigorian, *The Emergence of Modern Afghanistan: The Politics of Reform and Modernization 1880-1946* (Stanford, CA: Stanford University Press, 1969), 46-49. The system of *jagirdari* (also transliterated as *jagirdari*) worked in the *qalang* areas vice the *nang*. A *sardar* (also transliterated as *sirdar*) is a military title roughly equating to earl or count that was used primarily by Durrani Pashtuns. It was later used as a title for male members of the Afghan royal family.

[48]Elphinstone, *An Account of the Kingdom of Caubul,* 544; Regarding bodyguards: Olaf Caroe, *The Pathans* (1958; repr., Karachi, Pakistan: Union Book Stall, 1973), 256-262. Durrani established a

Using *jagirdari,* Durrani could counter rising rivals by fracturing their power base by awarding *jagirs* to their subordinates. Durrani recognized that by dealing with local *qawms* directly he could prevent aggregate groups from challenging him. At the same time, Durrani tapped into a sense of Pashtun nationalism by leading them in successful expeditions against non-Pashtuns. In this respect, he was able to retain power by an approach that encompassed both micro and macro identities.[49]

Ahmad Shah Durrani's nascent dynasty exceeded the constructs of Pashtun tribal governance, and it was not advantageous for him to strictly follow Pashtun customs as it would dilute his power and autonomy. In response, Durrani imported bureaucratic systems from the Persian Safavid Empire that he had observed while serving under Nadir Shah. His son, Timur Shah, extended this in 1775 when he moved the capital to Kabul and employed many non-Pashtuns to run the government, much to the chagrin of Pashtun tribal leaders.[50] To broaden his supra-tribal support, he promoted the concept of a larger Afghan identity and common religious heritage. The common religion was also a method for Durrani to set up state-run religious courts that existed outside the limits of the tribe, both unifying the disparate groups and extending his personal influence. He also established ties with rival tribes by taking wives from them, a tradition of identity bonding that extended into the 20th Century.[51]

---

personal bodyguard known as the *Ghulamishah,* or "King's Slaves." Rather than relying on kinsmen, the *Ghulamishah* was composed of fierce Qizilbashi tribesmen, Turkmen Shi'a warriors loyal only to the king.

[49]Rubin, *The Fragmentation of Afghanistan,* 46.

[50]Dupree, 340-341. Though he took actions to reduce the power of the Durrani Pashtuns vis-á-vis his own, Ahmad Shah Durrani would also show them great respect and deference as well as consult them on matters of governance. His son, Timur Shah, had a much more contentious relationship, either because he did so much to isolate them from power or as a result of it. These included his movement of the capitol to Kabul, his employment of the Qizilbashi bodyguard, and the incorporation of Tajiks into the government.

[51]Grigorian, 48-49. Regarding politically based polygamy into the 20th Century: Barnett R. Rubin, "A Tribe Apart: Afghan Elites Face a Corrosive Past," *Boston Review* (January/February 2009), http://bostonreview net/BR34.1/rubin.php (accessed March 15, 2009).

Durrani's control of Afghanistan was not ubiquitous. The *jagirdari* system worked in the *hukumat* or areas where there was a patron-client relationship among the elites. In the *yaghistan* areas where leadership was non-enduring, dynamic, and ephemeral, such systems were anathema.[52] The Ghilzai tribal confederation, which predominately lived in the mountainous region along today's Afghanistan-Pakistan border, had a long standing feud with the Durrani branch prior to Ahmad Shah Durrani's rise to power. Though he conducted numerous expeditions against non-Pashtuns, his greatest battles were against his fellow Pashtuns, the Ghilzai.[53] The new king understood the limits of his ability to control these independent factions. He never attempted to assume administrative control over these remote regions and even paid tolls to the Afridi and Shinwari Pashtun tribes of the Khyber region to facilitate trade and allow safe passage.[54]

Analysis

Ahmad Shah Durrani's rise to power was significant due to his ability to mobilize the Pashtun tribes and create a working tribal confederation beyond the limits of his specific tribe and subtribe. Under his leadership, new systems of governance were employed. These were extended greatly (though less successfully) by his successor, Timur Shah. Durrani was able to secure loyalty through the *jagirdari* system, and the management of how much power subordinates and

---

[52]The term *yaghistan* was coined after this period during the rule of Abdur Rahman (1880-1901) though it is conceptually valid at this point. The dynamics between settled societies and remote border tribes was detailed extensively in Ibn Khaldun's 13th century text, *The Muqaddimah* and is referenced by many scholars describing this friction. In addition to its long-standing antipathy toward the Durrani tribal confederation, the Ghilzai would not submit to the long-standing arrangement of *jagirdari*. First of all, they did not recognize Durrani's authority to make such grants, as that would be an infringement on their long-standing autonomy. Second, Durrani could not effectively enforce the obedience of these tribes.

[53]It is important to note that these are not monolithic divisions. There were some elements of the Ghilzais that sided with Ahmad Shah Durrani, as well as Durrani tribes that were not under his domain, though they shared some kinship ties. Any generalization about groups in Afghanistan--by ethnicity, tribal affiliation, religion, or otherwise--is bound to have its exceptions.

[54]Caroe, 258.

potential rivals could muster. Even so, Durrani's rule was tenuous, both among his supposed Durrani Pashtun allies as well as the traditional rivals in the ungoverned spaces. There is a useful metaphor to describe the nature of state control in the Durrani dynasty--the state as a source of light. Rather than being defined by specific boundaries, the power of the state was like a light source, strongest near the seat of the ruler and weaker as you move farther away from it. Legitimacy was strictly determined by the able to control, whether through appeasement or coercion. In the ungoverned edges, the "light" of Durrani's power was dim or non-existent.[55]

With regards to ethnic groups, Durrani's impact was primarily on the Pashtun and the establishment of the Durrani confederation on a path to hegemony over most Afghan government functions up until the coup of 1978. Though more so as conquests than primary players, the Hazara, Tajik, Uzbek, Punjab, Qizilbashi, and Sikh societies were deeply affected by the expanding Durrani dynasty, with the Tajiks and the Qizilbashi playing more and more of a significant role in government toward the end of Durrani's rule and under the rule of his son, Timur Shah. From this point on, these different groups had a hand, albeit marginal, in Afghan government.

The importance of local social structures cannot be disregarded. Durrani was able to organize the various *qawms* to meet his ends. He did this by meeting their needs in accordance with their tribal structures. Additionally, he developed the beginnings of a national Afghan/Pashtun identity which he used to great success in conquests outside of Pashtun areas. Durrani also used the religion of Islam as a unifying identity to counter the reticence of local *qawms* to his authority. He capitalized on incorporating permanent leverage on the *qawms* through intermarriage and establishing a patron-client relationship through *jagirs* and positions

---

[55]Jeffery Herbst, *States and Power in Africa: Comparative Lessons in Authority and Control* (Princeton, NJ: Princeton University Press, 2000), 35-46. Though not novel in and of itself, the idea for this metaphor comes from Herbst's work. Though it discusses power relationships in post-colonial Africa, the concept is valid in pre-colonial Afghanistan.

within the government. Most notably, he prevented *qawms* from uniting to counter him by engaging at the local level to prevent rival power bases and not attempting over extending his authority into the ungovernable *nang* areas. Much of this was accomplished because Durrani secured a sufficient inflow of capital to finance his efforts, specifically by the subjugation of rich non-Pashtun lands of the Mughal Empire to the east. Durrani's techniques for control are a common theme among successful central governments in Afghanistan.

The Great Game Era

The Great Game was the imperialist competition between Czarist Russia and Great Britain. Britain's first involvement with Afghanistan began with the arrival of Mountstuart Elphinstone, the "pioneer of Afghan anthropology," in 1808.[56] As Russia expanded south through the Central Asian states, the British reaction was to develop Afghanistan as a buffer state to protect its interests in India.[57] The Great Game included the three Anglo-Afghan Wars. The First Anglo-Afghan War (1839-1842) was fought over Russian overtures to the Afghan government and resulted in the British emplacing a friendly ruler on the throne, the previously deposed Shah Shuja. It ended with an ignominious defeat of British forces, the death of Shah Shuja, and the starting of a new Durrani dynasty.[58] The Second Anglo-Afghan War (1878-1881) was fought

---

[56]Glatzer, "The Pashtun Tribal System," 265-282. Mountstuart Elphinstone, a political officer in the East India Company, was sent on a diplomatic mission in October 1808 to the court in Kabul to persuade Shah Shuja to ally with England against a potential foray into Asia by Napoleon. Elphinstone had a long and distinguished career in India and was well respected. Ironically, his cousin, Major General William Keith Elphinstone, was the commander of the British Army annihilated at the close of the First Anglo-Afghan War. The dubbing of Elphinstone as the "pioneer of Afghan Anthropology" appears in Glatzer, though any serious work on Afghanistan's history will reference Elphinstone.

[57]Rubin, *The Fragmentation of Afghanistan*, 8, 47.

[58]Heathcote, 46-66. The 4,500 man garrison of Kabul, along with approximately 10,000 family members and camp followers, attempted to escape to Jalalabad. The British envoy, Sir William MacNaghten, had secured a peace treaty with some prominent *sardars*, but other powerful khans and *sardars* refused to recognize the validity of the treaty. When MacNaghten clumsily tried to trick the Pashtun tribal leaders, he was ambushed and assassinated shortly before the British began their withdrawal. Ghilzai tribes, along with Afridis and even Durranis nominally allied with the ruler, constantly attacked the

over roughly similar circumstances--Russian overtures to the Afghan government and British efforts to impose its will upon the government of Afghanistan to prevent Russian influence. This war also had a fairly ignominious end for the British, but was not altogether non-beneficial. The British Raj did consolidate land gains, and the post-conflict turmoil in Afghanistan resulted in the rise of a monarch who indirectly accomplished British objectives. This monarch was Amir Abdur Rahman Khan--the "Iron Amir."[59] The Great Game between Russia and Britain ended with the Third Anglo-Afghan War (1919), where a war-weary Britain ended the month-long conflict with the Treaty of Rawalpindi and removed itself from Afghan affairs.[60]

The First Anglo-Afghan War was the first example of a Western government falling into the trap of trying to impose a foreign form of governance in an environment in Afghanistan that it woefully misunderstood. The British placed Shah Shuja as their proxy on the throne not realizing he lacked legitimacy in the eyes of the people and the local elites. The opinions of the "subjects" of the pretender are summed up in this quote by Nawab Jubbar Khan, a Durrani *sardar* who negotiated terms with the British as they planned their withdrawal from Kabul, "If Shah Shuja really is a King and come to the kingdom of his ancestors, what is the use of your army and name. You have brought him, by your money and arms, into Afghanistan. Leave him now with us Afghans, and let him rule us if he can."[61] The British imposed their form of bureaucracy on the government, gutting the existing "corrupt" and "inefficient" systems, not realizing that these very

---

retreating party resulting in mass slaughter. Only one British soldier, Assistant Surgeon William Brydon, escaped alive to Jalalabad. Of note, many other Britons were captured and later repatriated.

[59]Amir Abdur Rahman Khan is also referred to in various sources as Abdur Rahman and Abdurrahman.

[60]Heathcote, 189-205. The Treaty of Rawalpindi was signed on August 8, 1919 after minimal fighting. The British had achieved limited tactical victory, repelling Afghan forces who had entered India and using airpower to punish the Afghan government. The terms were essentially dictated by the British, including the reaffirmation of the Durand Line and the divesture of British's authority to conduct Afghan foreign affairs.

[61]Heathcote, 42.

systems form the relationships with the local *qawms* and provided the power and authority to the king. Even as British forces were withdrawing from Kabul, their agreements were with the powerless central authority, not with the independent *qawms* who controlled the route of their departure. Amongst the competing *qawms*, the only thing that they could agree on was the imposition of the foreign British element and their shared rejection of it.[62]

The Second Anglo-Afghan War occurred in much the same way as the first. Russia used internal turmoil within Afghanistan to extend inroads to the embattled government. Britain objected to the expanding Russian influence and attempted to counter this by direct military action. Though there were shared goals between the Afghan government and Britain, a series of misunderstandings and incoherent guidance from the British government led to the interjection of British forces. Though they departed eventually, the British did secure concrete territorial gains-- which would turn into a source of continued conflict later on. The exacerbated internal conflict in Afghanistan allowed a powerful new Amir to come to the throne, Amir Abdur Rahman Khan. For the next 21 years, he conducted a campaign of "internal imperialism."[63]

Amir Abdur Rahman succeeded in uniting the *qawms* in more ways than one. He was the first to declare the divine right of kings in Afghanistan and invoked Islam to consolidate power to a much more substantial degree than Durrani.[64] He promulgated state-run *sharia* courts to arbitrate between *qawms,* effectively extending his personal authority. In line with this, he also

---

[62]Ibid, 42-46.

[63]From an external state-based perspective, this makes sense. From within, it truly was extension of the authority of the government. Afghan kings lacked the authority that the state system assumed that they had. Abdur Rahman, more effectively than most, but still not completely, seized that authority in much the same way that Ahmad Shah Durrani did.

[64]Saikal, 35. Ahmad Shah Durrani also used Islam as a unifying factor, claiming the title of Defender of the Faith and rallying support of Muslims to fight. Abdur Rahman went far beyond this with an Islamic version of the divine right of kings as justification for his authority and as a mandate for action.

used the Islamic mandate to punish "heretics"--the Shi'a Hazara and Kafirs of Kafiristan.[65] He also mimicked and expanded on Durrani's technique of diffusing potential rivals through the policy of "Afghanisation"--dissipation of rival Pashtun groups by forcibly moving them from traditional Pashtun tribal areas and relocating them to areas dominated by different ethnic groups.[66] This reduced the powerful blocks of rival Pashtun tribes as well as that of ethnic rivals. The Iron Amir also secured compliance by the practice of *ghulam-bachah,* the keeping of sons of potential rivals in his court, ostensibly to train them in the roles of government, but in practical terms as hostages to ensure compliance with his wishes. Additionally, Abdur Rahman also took wives to build loyalty bonds with various influential *qawms.*[67]

What was so notable about Abdur Rahman's approach was how complicit the British were in supporting his actions. He was directly subsidized in this campaign by the British Raj. By aiding a strong central government in Afghanistan, though it may have been contrary to British ideals, achieved the purpose of providing the buffer between India and Russia. Amir Abdur Rahman's agenda was enabled by direct British financial support vice Durrani's conquest of foreign lands, in essence providing the same effect--the means to consolidate power. While

---

[65]Saikal, 36. This small enclave had resisted the spread of Islam up until this point. Abdur Rahman forcibly converted them. The area known as Kafiristan was renamed Nuristan--The Land of Light--and retains that name today. Nuristan, as well as Hazara areas, is notorious for defying central authority whenever possible.

[66]Saikal, 38-9; Bleuer, "'Afghanisation:' a Rather Unfortunate Neologism." Though Abdur Rahman was wary of British interference, he was more concerned with Russian encroachment from the north. He was suspicious of non-Pashtun ethnic groups in the north. His British advisors advocated the program where he split rival Ghilzai power bases in the Pashtun belt by relocating them to the Tajik and Uzbek areas of the north through coercion or brute force in most cases. The end result was a form of ethnic cleansing of what he saw as potential political and military threats both inside and outside the Pashtun community.

[67]On *ghulam-bachah,* see Dupree, *Afghanistan,* 188. Regarding Abdur Rahman's wives, see Saikal, *Modern Afghanistan,* 39, and Dupree, *Afghanistan,* 428-9.

Abdur Rahman maintained a façade of fierce independence, his signing of the 1893 Durand Agreement demonstrates that he was beholden to a degree to the British government.[68]

Given the fairly spectacular nature of the first and second conflicts in Afghanistan, the Third Anglo-Afghan War was fairly anticlimactic. The changing strategic nature as well the exhaustion of the British Empire of through World War I resulted in the end of the Third Anglo-Afghan War only few months after fighting began. With the signing of the Treaty of Rawalpindi, Britain reaffirmed the borders of Afghanistan and ended both its subsidization of Afghanistan and its dominion over Afghan foreign affairs. Though this ended the Great Game, international affairs would continue to have a profound impact on Afghanistan's internal politics.[69]

---

[68]The Durand Agreement established the Durand Line, the "scientific" border between Afghanistan and the British Raj, and by extension modern day Pakistan. Per Elphinstone, one thing the king was not able to do was to forfeit tribal lands. But 80 years later, that is what he effectively did. (Abdur Rahman's autobiography demurs, saying that it was merely an ascription of supervisory authority given temporarily to the Raj, not a permanent divesture of Pashtun lands.) This split the tribal lands of various Pashtun tribes. To the *nang* tribes that lived in the area, which did not ascribe to the authority of the Afghan king, nor to the Raj, life continued as before. Attempts to demarcate the border were met with the characteristic violence of the area. It was never effectively done. The line existed on the map, but was not particularly relevant outside of interstate diplomatic channels. With the exception of the Khyber Pass and the southern route through Chaman, where land lines of communications existed, there was no issue. In these locations, the local tribes still had to be bribed to ensure safe passage, the Pashtun version of a protection racket and a local source of income. When Britain divested itself from the Indian subcontinent, it held a referendum to determine what form of government would represent the areas. The choices were between a secular government (present day India) and an Islamic government (Pakistan, including what was then known as East Pakistan, which split in 1971 to form independent Bangladesh). Afghanistan argued that a third option should have been made available to the Pashtun populace on the east side of the Durand Line--joining Afghanistan. Afghanistan declared that the Durand Line had been illegally settled between the British Raj and Amir Abdur Rahman and claimed the Pashtun lands (Pakistan's Northwest Frontier Province and the Federally Administered Tribal Areas), as well as the province of Baluchistan, as part of Afghanistan, specifically "Pashtunistan." Pakistan, with a multivariate ethnic population, saw this as an existential threat; it touted its status as a Muslim nation that subsumed ethnic identity. The issue was always contentious, resulting in outright border conflict at times, though not as profound as the conflicts with India over Jammu and Kashmir. With the loss of East Pakistan in 1971, the relative value of the Pashtun tribal lands increased. The friendly relations between India and Afghanistan were also seen as a threat, which played a hand in Pakistan's motivations and methods as the influence of communism crept into Afghanistan. See Caroe, *The Pathans*, 381-3, 419, 436; Roy, *Islam and Resistance in Afghanistan*, 71, 76, 211; Dupree, *Afghanistan*, 423-429.

[69]Heathcote, 166-205. Heathcote gives a balanced perspective of the Third Anglo-Afghan War in the Chapters, "The Kings Move" and "The End Game" of *The Afghan Wars*. After the exhaustion of World War I and the sea change in Russia with the creation of the Soviet Union, Afghanistan's perceived relative importance shifted greatly. See also Dupree, *Afghanistan*, 430-441.

Analysis

The presence of foreign forces and external intervention by the British in the First and Second Anglo-Afghan Wars was an anathema to the disparate populace who bound together in common purpose to repel the invaders. Though there was internecine conflict before and after, the divergent groups shared one thing: violent reaction to the *fehrengi* or foreigners.[70] By providing the disparate *qawms* with a common enemy, it allowed them to unite to fight the British. The will of the local groups at times even exceeded the capacity of high-level Afghan officials to control them. Projecting beyond the Great Game, this trait can be seen again with the Soviet intervention in Afghanistan. To a degree, even the Taliban form of government was rejected, though not with the unity that rallied the Afghan people against the infidels. While many outsiders looking in see the Taliban as natural Afghan government, they were in many ways to many *qawms* just another external aggressor, though the fact that they were Muslim may have dampened the reaction of the people.[71]

The British government succeeded in meeting its goals when it did so through an accepted power structure within Afghanistan, most notably Abdur Rahman Khan. There are parallels in future instances as well. The Soviets, before the Soviet-Afghan War and after, were

---

[70]The term *fehrengi*, also commonly transliterated as *ferengi* and *farangay,* equates to "foreigner" or "alien" in a number of Indo-Aryan languages, though there are number of purported etymologies. In Afghanistan it referred to Westerners in general and the British specifically.

[71]The idea that the Taliban was a popular movement among the Afghan people is one that has been countered from several corners. It found support around the anarchic area around Kandahar, but met resistance throughout most other areas of Afghanistan. In many part of Afghanistan, it pushed out much more effective forms of collective governance, including the governments of Ismail Khan in Heart, Abdul Rashid Dostum in Mazar e Sharif, and Bernuddin Rabbani in Kabul and the north. While some Pashtun saw it as a means to regain ethnic hegemony throughout Afghanistan, without the massive support of Pakistan, the Taliban would have never achieved what it did nor stayed as long as it did. Considering that the rule of the Taliban lasted only five years, it can be categorized with other foreign invaders. The Taliban's rapid collapse upon the start of OEF points to both its lack of legitimacy and lack of support among the Afghan populace. See Christian Bleuer, "The Persistent Myth of Pre-Taliban Anarchy," The Ghosts of Alexander: The Afghan Campaign, 2001 to Whenever, entry posted April 7, 2008, http://easterncampaign.word press.com/2007/04/24/the-persistent-myth-of-pre-taliban-anarchy/ (accessed February 27, 2009); Goodson, *Afghanistan's Endless War,* 124; Rashid, *Taliban,* 19, 33-34.

able to affect policy through the support to the government, though the goals were far from pervasive.[72] Additionally, the formation of the Taliban, its subsequent rise to power, and sustainment was largely due to external support of Pakistan through its shadowy Inter-Services Intelligence (ISI) directorate.[73]

Powerful central authority in Afghanistan depended upon control of the disparate *qawms*. Abdur Rahman successfully leveraged the power of the *qawms* through multiple means including a system of allegiance similar to the *jagirdari* system of Durrani and unifying themes such as Pashtun nationalism and Islam. Rahman also used some fairly nefarious means to maintain power, such as keeping hostages of various *qawms* at court, religious persecution, and ethnic

---

[72]A comprehensive treatment of the Soviet experience in Afghanistan well exceeds the limits of this paper, but some points are worth highlighting. From British disengagement from Afghanistan and later India and Pakistan, the Soviet influence spread to Afghanistan. Through various types of aid and assistance, Soviet influence spread to the urban centers and among the social, political, and military elites. Because of limited outlets for trade (given the status of relations with Pakistan), the Soviet Union became engrained in many facets of Afghanistan's society. This influence did not extend to the local *qawms*, however, as the more remote and traditional elements of the disparate Afghan society resisted wholesale change. As Soviet surrogates and Marxist elites within Afghanistan forced changes after a series of coups and repression of local leadership, the inability of the central government to effectively dictate change was exposed. Under the guise of an "invitation" and in attempt to stabilize and control the erratic Marxist elites in power, the Soviets invaded and met with the same combined reaction that the British did in their direct intervention. However, when the Soviets withdrew, the puppet government of Mohammad Najibullah lasted for three years with varying degrees of waning Soviet support. See M. Hassan Kakar, *Afghanistan,* 21-31, and Rubin, *The Fragmentation of Afghanistan,* 111-121.

[73]The dynamics of Afghanistan and Pakistan exceed the limits of this paper, but some points are illustrative. Pakistani influence in Afghan politics has occurred since Pakistan's creation in 1947 and exacerbated by Afghanistan's claims on Pashtunistan. As early as the 1970s, Pakistani military and ISI agents trained militants of various ethnic backgrounds in Pakistan for operations in Afghanistan. The central theme behind these militants was to support Islam against communist/western influences among the ruling elites (predominantly Pashtuns, who advocated the concept of a greater Pashtunistan). This began well before the Soviet invasion and foreshadowed the general scheme of Pakistani support during the Soviet-Afghan War. ISI controlled support to the *mujahidin* groups throughout the Soviet-Afghan War promoting radical Islamic groups ahead of nationalist groups, as that supported Pakistan's ends of identifying Islam ahead of ethnicity and countering potential nationalist conflicts that might emerge. After several years of infighting amongst the various *mujahidin* groups after the Soviet withdrawal, the ISI supported the fundamentalist Deobandi group, the Taliban, as a means to influence its western neighbor. It is not accurate to say that the Taliban were entirely subservient to the Pakistani government or the ISI, but it was largely a creation of them. See Sinno, "Explaining the Taliban's Ability to Mobilize the Pashtuns," 69-71; Roy, *Islam and Resistance in Afghanistan,* 71, 76; Rashid, *Taliban,* 1-17.

cleansing and forced migration. Unsavory aspects aside, Rahman's ability to wield power shows how Afghans can be united in both positive and negative ways.

In addition to understanding and manipulating identity groups, Abdur Rahman had external capital to support his government. Like Durrani, this was a necessary element in building a government. In the years that followed Britain's departure from Afghanistan, central Afghan governments were unable to retain the authority that they had in the past, the source of external support having dried up. The lesson to be extracted from this would be that this external funding, while necessary, is not sufficient to enact effective central governance. Looking at the Soviet example, one would see a massive expenditure that went awry as the central government strayed from its perceived legitimacy and outside of the bounds of efficacy. Similarly, the Taliban fell when the United States began OEF, as its message did not ring true with the bulk of Afghans. From this, one can posit that it is both a linkage of capital and legitimacy among the identity groups that are both needed if one hopes to affect governance in Afghanistan.

Conclusions and Recommendations

It would be impossible for this monograph to predict the future with any degree of certainty based on an evaluation of the past. The nature of the environment in Afghanistan is far too complex, and our ability to assess it is far too limited. However, the monograph can point to what might be plausible given the analysis of the selected eras. The analysis of the two case studies illustrated how the disparate ethnic groups and the local *qawms* reacted to and were influenced by the different governmental systems. Ahmad Shah Durrani used these groupings to his advantage, understanding how they functioned, what would work, and what would not. He achieved his goals by knowing how to engage these groups. But he also understood what he could not accomplish, what resources were required, and how to use both positive and negative means to accomplish his goals. During the Great Game, foreign powers came to Afghanistan and attempted to assert their will. With a lack of understanding, the disparate *qawms* and ethnic groups reacted negatively and violently to British and Russian efforts. In that same era, Afghanistan experienced the very effective and relatively unifying rule of Amir Abdur Rahman. Though Abdur Rahman ruled in a decidedly different manner than Ahmad Shah Durrani and incorporated many aspects of Western governance in his reign, his success was inextricably linked with Durrani's in that it was based on understanding the dynamics of the local groups as well as the limits of his power. However, perhaps the most illustrative point for modern formulators of strategy is that many of the British goals that they had been unable to affect through direct intervention were accomplished through conditional and discrete support to Amir Abdur Rahman. While the aftermath of some of these machinations is still being felt, there are some lessons to be extracted from these two eras. The lessons learned can be categorized under two broad categories--the Afghan conception of identity and sources of power.

Identity

The role personal and local identity plays in determining the future of Afghanistan is immense, but Western efforts fail to get a coherent picture of that identity. Looking at the "Afghan" populace as one distinct and monolithic body is inaccurate and dangerous. The truth of the matter is that there is not just one, nor are there only fifty. The scope of Afghan identity is dynamic and must be applied in the context to be useful. It defies a simple, flat description.

The common conception of the Afghan individual, as constructed by an outsider, consists of an amalgamation of many, many different societies combined together. By analogy, one could describe a five gallon block of ice and a five gallon pot of boiling water collectively as ten gallons of water with an average temperature of 106 degree Fahrenheit. While that description may have a degree of technical accuracy, it is misleading and not particularly useful to someone who is making decisions based on that information. When observers fail to closely consider the context of the "Afghan" population being dealt with at the point of interaction, they make the same mistake, metaphorically placing a hand into that pot of boiling water. While there are reports of nascent feelings of an Afghan national ethos, it is important to not count on this budding sense of Afghan identity as a given rather than an emergent potential for future development.[74]

The "water temperature" analogy, while illustrative of the basic flaws in lumping Afghans together, fails to capture the dynamic and complex interaction of reality. More than hot or cold, the interaction of these disparate groups depends on the scale at which you regard them. A Barakzai Pashtun will respond differently to otherwise identical challenges from a kinsman, a Ghilzai Pashtun, a Tajik, an ethnically different Muslim, or a Westerner. At some level, each can be regarded as an opponent, even though each may also have a degree of shared identity and common interest. The issue of personal identity is of extreme importance in Afghanistan, but it is also dynamic and defies definition in a discrete taxonomy. The role of identity in the Afghan persona is also directly related to the formulation of Afghan power structures.

Power Structures

Power in Afghanistan differs from Western conceptions in several ways. It is locally based, with sovereignty remaining with the individual or the *qawm*. The rule of law is a fairly novel concept in many areas, and simple declaration of that law is insufficient to convince the populace of the validity that law. Additionally, a *qawm* will not accept change in governance unless it is compelled to do so, or it sees that the change is in line with its interests. Finally, effective central governments in Afghanistan have historically required outside resources to exert control within their domain.

First of all, power, authority, and legitimacy in Afghanistan originate at the local level. Even among groups who might have a propensity to accept reified centralized authority

---

[74]Bernt Glatzer, "War and Boundaries in Afghanistan: Significance and Relativity of Local and Social Boundaries," *Die Welt des Islams* 41, no. 3 (2001): 379-399, http://www.ag-afghanistan.de/files/war-a-bound.pdf (accessed October 2, 2008)

structures, for example the *qalang* Pashtuns, abstract and absent authority is no authority at all. From Durrani's era, centralized authority was based on his connection with these smaller groups and playing them against one another, making their interests tied to support. Even so, Durrani's authority was not ubiquitous, it was the result of his efforts to co-opt, cajole, and even coerce the groups. Without the mechanisms in place, his ability to rule would have been nil. Even as such, his authority was based on his real and perceived ability to enforce it, not by a mandate or government of laws.

Second, authority is not historically rooted in the rule of law as envisioned by Western governments. It resides in what is accepted by the group identity, the *qawm*. When a foreign power comes in, as in the example of the British during the Great Game and later the Soviets, the Taliban, and coalition forces now, and dictates rules, they come with no sense of legitimacy or authority. While the Taliban had the shared identity of being Muslim and, with a large segment of the population, being Pashtun, they were still not effective in controlling the tightly knit *qawms* that maintained independent identity. Therefore, declaring authority in a matter is one thing, convincing fiercely independent groups of that authority is quite another. Without the acquiescence of the population, abstract central authority is ineffective. Without the needs of these groups being met, they see no incentive for participation in government or acceptance of the government's sovereignty. For a large number of these groups, independence from foreign control is the basis of their entire history and culture. For most of the remainder, the recent history has been the interjection of foreign powers acting outside their best interests. While the rule of law may be in the best interests of the various *qawms*, this is hard to visualize given the traditions of patron-client relationships and might makes right policy.

Finally, the case studies show that both Durrani and Abdur Rahman gained their decisive advantage by being able to mobilize capital that their predecessors could not. Durrani had it in the form of the treasure of Nadir Shah and the spoils of conquered lands. Abdur Rahman had it in the money paid to him by the British Raj in exchange for favorable policy decisions and for providing a buffer between India and the Russians. With these resources, each was able to manipulate the state structure to his advantage. Beyond the case studies, this can be seen in the experiences of the various Afghan regimes supported by the Soviets (when the Soviets were not intervening directly in the country), the Taliban supported by the ISI of Pakistan, and the Karzai government supported by the UN, ISAF, and the United States. While the efficacy and legitimacy of these regimes can be brought into question, they have never been viable at all without heavy foreign support.

In dealing with a complex situation such as the current state of affairs in Afghanistan, the proper appreciation of the culture and the context is critical. Having explored the diversity among the Afghan populace and the sources of power and legitimacy in Afghanistan, this discourse concludes with recommendations for further study and possible action.

Recommendations

This monograph points to two key areas that need further study. The first is to determine the true U.S. interests in Afghanistan. The second is to conduct a critical examination of Afghan governance with respect to the expectations of its populace. Concomitant with these two areas is the continued study of past and present Afghan culture to better inform the strategic, operational, and tactical decision makers involved in development, implementing, and evaluating policy in Afghanistan. The "intimate knowledge" of the situation is absolutely necessary to making informed decisions. Without that, decisions are based on abstract doctrinal approaches that may not be congruent with the true nature of the environment. Central Asian expert Joshua Foust explains "When looking at Afghanistan through Afghanistan, rather than any pre-designed

Western conceptions of warfighting, you get a wholly different idea of what an appropriate strategy for the country would entail. We would do well to remember that."[75]

The most critical area for further study is the nature, priority, and congruence of U.S. goals in Afghanistan. This subject is particularly sensitive in that it is far from academic only, and has an inextricable political aspect to it. The United States entered Afghanistan as part of a rapidly developed effort to counter al Qaeda terrorists and the Taliban government that protected them. The mission has evolved to one of establishing acceptable governance, promoting democratic values, and countering the various components of a multi-faceted insurgency. The question that must be examined is how these new goals tie back to the core interests of the United States. In unveiling the new strategic approach for the United States in Afghanistan, President Barack Obama directly stated the "clear and focused goal: to disrupt, dismantle and defeat al Qaeda in Pakistan and Afghanistan, and to prevent their return to either country in the future. That's the goal that must be achieved. That is a cause that could not be more just."[76] While the goal is clearly stated, the logic that connects the goal and its subordinate objectives to the national interest was based in a Western-biased mindset that is incongruent with the context of the environment in which it must be applied. The logic proposed is that by achieving the goals for Afghan governance and fighting al Qaeda in Afghanistan, the threat of terrorism by al Qaeda and other terrorist organizations is decreased. It does not account for the reaction of the Afghan people to these efforts. Additionally, if the United States is "fixing" Afghanistan to deny al Qaeda a safe-haven, logic and precedent have established a requirement for the United States to "fix" the next place that al Qaeda lands, currently Pakistan and inevitably another inhospitable location

---

[75]Joshua Foust, "What 'Intimate Knowledge?'" Registan.com, entry posted September 29, 2008, http://www registan net/index.php/2008/09/29/quote-of-the-day-8/ (accessed April 19, 2009).

[76]President, Remarks, "A New Strategy for Afghanistan and Pakistan," White House Press Office, March 27, 2009, http://www.whitehouse.gov/the_press_office/Remarks-by-the-President-on-a-New-Strategy-for-Afghanistan-and-Pakistan/ (accessed May 1, 2009).

after that.[77] Also, if the United States defines the success of the government of Afghanistan as critical to American interests, it has effectively tied the prestige and resources of the nation to achieving that goal. Given that qualification, there is not a compelling incentive for the supported Afghan government to change. If the United States categorizes the conflict in Afghanistan as a "no fail" situation, then it has obligated itself to stay and win, regardless of the costs. The converse of this would be to quit the region and turn the situation into a strategic defeat. Neither is a particularly appealing scenario, especially if the true U.S. interests in the region are not truly critical. However, if the U.S. Government declares that it is a U.S. interest that the government of Afghanistan thrives, but not an essential one, the calculus changes. In such a situation, the United States could qualify its level of support and put conditions on its assistance. Making this linkage more ephemeral and tenuous, it has potentially created a strong impetus for the government of Afghanistan to both work toward maintaining positive relations with the world power that is not obligated to stay and gain support from its populace and legitimacy in their eyes. There is an element of the unknown in this path, and it does not guarantee success. But qualifying the essentiality of the United States' interest affects the dynamics of the situation immensely.

The first area of examination was based on defining U.S. policy. This one is based on the efficacy of the Afghan government itself. The current government of Afghanistan, created in the vacuum that followed Taliban misrule, is modeled on external Western perceptions of governance. In this construct, authority is held at the center and distributed downward. Regardless of the merits of the democratic process and the rule of law ostensibly incorporated with this new government, this manifestation of government is diametrically opposed to the historical role,

---

[77]Andrew Exum, "Andrew Exum on The Rachel Maddow Show," abu Muqawawa, entry posted April 4, 2009, http://abumuqawama.blogspot.com/2009/04/andrew-exum-on-rachel-maddow html (accessed April 6, 2009). Andrew Exum, a fellow at the Center for New American Security, argued the point that by establishing the precedent of "fixing" states where al Qaeda seeks refuge, the United States is going down a slippery slope of what the nation can physically and morally accomplish to eliminate terrorist threats.

accepted boundaries, and granted authority of government institutions in Afghanistan. Given the isolated nature of Afghanistan and the fierce self-reliance instilled in the disparate *qawms*, this usurpation of power is logically viewed with suspicion and resisted when possible. While this new form of government may benefit some people and some *qawms*, others will (rightly) view it as an existential threat to the identity that is central to their way of life. As the *qawms* will not willingly accept a central government that does not serve its interests, a critical area for continued study is how to foster a government that has the authority, resources, and legitimacy to exercise sovereign rule over these disparate groups.

Beyond these areas for further study, there are three actions that will better address cultural context depicted in the monograph. First, adjust the planning horizon of the conflict. Second, reduce the signature of coalition forces. Finally, make support conditional, though this action does come with caveats.

In *Resisting Rebellion,* author Anthony Joes recalls a cliché about the U.S. military effort in Vietnam, "the U.S. did not fight a ten-year war in Vietnam; it fought a one-year war ten times."[78] There is a sad truth to that statement which can be applied to the current U.S. efforts in Afghanistan. Consider when the United States became actively involved in Afghanistan. U.S. intervention began soon after the Soviets invaded in 1979, thirty years ago.[79] In the interim, U.S. policy has alternately actively engaged with Afghanistan and Pakistan and completely abandoned them. There is credence in the claims that the situation in Afghanistan is related in large part to

---

[78]Anthony James Joes, *Resisting Rebellion: The History and Politics of Counterinsurgency* (Lexington, KY: University of Kentucky Press, 2004), 176.

[79]The United States became involved with Afghanistan even earlier than that, though covert assistance to the nascent *mujahidin* forces serves a clear benchmark for the beginning of military involvement. The first tangible evidence of U.S. involvement occurred on January 9, 1980, a month after the Soviet invasion, with a statement by Senator Birch Bayh, then Chairman of the Senate Select Committee on Intelligence, on NBC's *Today Show*: "we did take certain steps to help them [the Afghan resistance] do what any group of citizens should be able to do in a country." Newspaper articles soon after carried articles claiming the shipment of arms to the *mujahidin*. J. Bruce Amstutz, *Afghanistan: The First Five Years of Soviet Occupation* (Washington, DC: National Defense University Press, 1986), 199-200.

generational failures and inconsistencies in U.S. policy. The rotations of tactical and operational units have strategic implications as objectives shift and change with the personalities. However, the inability to maintain a coherent strategy is based on the failure to maintain a coherent policy, a direct result of the failure to realize and apply the true interests of the United States as mentioned earlier. Though tactical planning--both military and civilian--requires a degree of immediacy and proximity, for success they must be based in long term policy goals. The planning horizon must be 20 years, not 20 months, and it must expand beyond the boundaries of the current conflict. While these plans can be developed by professional military officers and diplomats, they are dependent on the discipline of elected government to support and adapt them only in the context of a long-term perspective vice short-term pressure and political expedience. Given the nature of the United States' political system, there will always be a degree of friction in achieving this. This does not change the necessity of such an outlook.

The second recommendation for action is to reduce the signature of coalition forces in Afghanistan. This does not necessarily mean reduce the coalition presence. In many respects, the coalition non-military coalition presence needs to increase. There is a truism that the United States is not a nation at war, but a military at war and a nation at the mall. Ambassador Ryan Crocker refined this sentiment that "not only is the nation not at war, but the government is not at war," referring to lack of capacity of non-Department of Defense government agencies to fill needed non-military roles in Afghanistan and Iraq.[80] By deferring interagency effort to military means, the signature of coalition forces in Afghanistan is immense. Considering the experiences of foreign military forces during the Great Game Era through the Taliban, the local societies of Afghanistan have uniformly reacted negatively to coercive intervention from outsiders. However,

---

[80] Ambassador Ryan Crocker (lecture, U.S. Army Command and General Staff College, Fort Leavenworth, Kansas, April 23, 2009. Guests at the Command and General Staff College normally speak in a non-attribution forum to allow for candid dialogue. However, Ambassador Crocker's address and follow-on question and answer session was specifically on the record.

foreign advisors have been consistently and successfully incorporated in Afghan military units and government agencies with minimal resistance. Given this evidence, the emphasis of foreign presence should be the advisory effort for the strategic effects of building government capacity and enhancing legitimacy within Afghanistan, even at the potential detriment of tactical setback. The question of true U.S. interests and their respective priorities must be considered and the rationale behind employment of forces adjusted to make this shift. With the example of airstrikes, the relative value of the targets must be compared with the impacts of visible foreign intervention and the perceptions of illegitimacy and impotency of the Afghan government created by these strikes. By reducing the signature of its military forces, both in terms of presence and effects, the United States and its coalition partners can reduce the unity of the disparate *qawms* in reaction. When OEF began, the Taliban collapsed because they were the focal point for Afghan anger. If the coalition presence becomes less pervasive, it gives the various insurgent groups, be they Taliban, warlords, drug runners, etcetera, the opportunity to become the focal point for Afghan reaction. Either they will be then rejected or they will adapt to meet the needs of the people in a manner accepted by them as legitimate.

Finally, the United States must make continued assistance to the Afghan government conditional. Carte blanche support provides no impetus for the Afghan government to make the changes necessary to achieve legitimacy in the eyes of its populace and the world community. This argument ties back to the true interests of the United States and obligations therein. This recommendation comes with two critical caveats. One, the conditions of the support must be acceptable to the Afghan *qawms* and feasible for the Afghan government. The Western prism of governance cannot be the sole standard, and the moral prescriptions of the West cannot be uncritically applied to a sovereign state. Second, support is not a binary, yes-or-no provision, nor is it synonymous with engagement. Setting "all or nothing" conditions is a recipe for failure because it prevents a flexible approach in the emergent development of relations. Additionally, the results of total disengagement from Afghanistan after the Soviet departure proved to be a primary factor in it devolving to the state that triggered OEF. Ambassador Crocker, speaking on the future of relations between the United States and both Afghanistan and Pakistan, stated that the United States must "stay the course" in relations with these two countries. When asked if he was suggesting unqualified support for the current regimes, Ambassador Crocker clarified that the important elements of the engagement strategy would be to serve as a reliable and enduring ally, focusing on shared interests; representing the values of the United States while not mandating them; and remaining engaged to understand the context of the Afghan and Pakistani states regardless of physical support. Ambassador Crocker highlighted the schizophrenic reversals of policy by decade from the 1960s until today in the region as confusing and unhelpful. With such drastic changes, U.S. support is viewed with suspicion by many in the region.[81] Again, this ties back to first point about clarifying U.S. interests and long-term strategy in the region. Again, one unavoidable obstacle to achieving this is the erratic nature of United States politics. This will be the impediment in composing and implementing policy in the future.

By considering the context of Afghanistan and the conclusions the monograph reached, exploring the areas for further study, and implementing the recommended actions, the United States and its coalition partners can develop a feasible, acceptable, and suitable strategy that will lead to satisfactory resolution of current conflict and a positive future. The monograph underscored the contextual importance of the dynamic Afghan social identity structures--the *qawms*--and the emergent power structures in the Durrani Empire and the Great Game Era. Identity in Afghanistan is dynamic and multi-faceted. While it can be based along tribal, ethnic,

---

[81]Crocker. The author asked the question in response to Ambassador Crocker's specific comment about "staying the course" with regards to engagement with governments of Afghanistan and Pakistan. The point of the question was how to balance this prescription with the United States' past history in supporting illegitimate regimes uncritically to the detriment of future relations with these countries when the regimes were replaced with unfriendly regimes, for example: Cuba, Nicaragua, and Iran. Ambassador Crocker acknowledged that support cannot be uncritical, but emphasized the need to be a "steady and reliable ally" focused on common interests, referencing how erratic diplomatic relations have had long term detrimental effects.

or linguistic lines, the strongest factor tends to be location. Even so, Afghans can have multiple identity affiliations which in turn translates to the ability to come together to resist foreign intervention. Power structures in Afghanistan are locally based, with authority being based in customary law such as *Pashtunwali* and the ability to influence vice rule of law. In the cases considered, external resources provided the means for strong rulers to exert authority over the *qawms*.

Given the conclusions, the author recommends two specific areas for further study, the true nature of U.S. interests in Afghanistan and the acceptability of Afghanistan's central government a legitimate sovereign authority, and the continued exploration of multiple facets of Afghan culture. In examining the nature of U.S. interests, it is important to go beyond the rhetoric and consider the core American interests at stake and how Afghanistan impacts them. Additionally, the study of how the current manifestation of Afghan governance is or is not congruent with varying perceptions of legitimacy of the social groups is a critical area of further study. This is a key and essential means of considering Afghanistan from the Afghan prism, in all actuality a multiplicity of intersecting and opposing viewpoints. An ongoing area of study needs to be context of Afghanistan's myriad cultures. The United States' military solution has thus far been reliant on technology and abstract doctrine. To succeed, the United States must develop an "intimate knowledge" of the environment.

Additionally, several actions can improve U.S. strategic prospects in Afghanistan. First and foremost, the U.S. government must adjust its planning horizon to fully consider the implication of its actions in a continuum. Strategy made without regard to a long-term approach and executed without the discipline to sustain that approach will be sporadic and ineffective. One year horizons have tactical and possibly operational implications; the twenty year perspective is strategic. Secondly, the United States and coalition must reduce the signature of its military, as this is an anathema to most of the Afghan populace. While advisor efforts can gain great benefits, coalition airstrikes provide a small tactical benefit at a great strategic cost. Embedded with a strategic view, these decisions will be readily apparent. Also, United States' efforts in Afghanistan need to expand beyond the military with a whole-of-government approach. Finally, support to Afghanistan cannot be uncritically given if the United States hopes to direct change in the country. Given this, support must not be couched as an all or nothing affair, but a means to exert influence through the provision of the external resources that have been critical to sustaining sovereign authority in Afghanistan. Also, regardless of direct support, continued engagement in Afghanistan is important in maintaining a metaphorical finger on the pulse of the state of affairs in that country and a mechanism for influence in the region. This last point may be the most important, as the past failures in doing so allowed Afghanistan to become the frustrating enigma that has challenged United States' efforts thus far.

BIBLIOGRAPHY

Books

Adamec, Ludwig W. *Dictionary of Afghan Wars, Revolutions, and Insurgencies.* Landham, MD: Scarecrow Press, 1996.

Amstutz, J. Bruce. *Afghanistan: The First Five Years of Soviet Occupation.* Washington, DC: National Defense University Press, 1986.

Caroe, Olaf. *The Pathans.* 1958. Reprint, Karachi, Pakistan: Union Book Stall, 1973.

Clausewitz, Carl von. *On War.* Edited and translated by Michael Howard and Peter Paret. Princeton, NJ: Princeton University Press, 1989.

Crews, Robert D., and Amin Tarzi, eds. *The Taliban and the Crisis of Afghanistan.* Cambridge, MA: Harvard University Press, 2008.

Dupree, Louis. *Afghanistan.* Rev. ed. Princeton, NJ: Princeton University Press, 1980.

Elphinstone, Mountstuart. *An Account of the Kingdom of Caubul: And Its Dependencies in Persia, Tartary, and India.*1815. Reprint, Whitefish, MT: Kessinger Publishing, 2008.

Giustozzi, Antonio. *War, Politics, and Society in Afghanistan: 1978-1992.*Washington, DC: Georgetown University Press, 2000.

Glatzer, Bernt. "Being Pashtun--Being Muslim: Concepts of Person and War in Afghanistan." In *Essays on South Asian Society: Culture and Politics II.* Berlin: Das Arabische Buch, 1998, 7. http://www.wardak.de/tribes/being_pashtun.pdf (accessed September 7, 2008).

————. "The Pashtun Tribal System." In *Concept of Tribal Society (Contemporary Society: Tribal Studies, Vol 5).* Edited by G. Pfeffer and D.K. Behera, 265-282. New Delhi: Concept Publishers, 2002.

Goodson, Larry P. *Afghanistan's Endless War: State Failure, Regional Politics, and the Rise of the Taliban.* Seattle, WA: University of Washington Press, 2001.

Grigorian, Vartan. *The Emergence of Modern Afghanistan: The Politics of Reform and Modernization 1880-1946.* Stanford, CA: Stanford University Press, 1969.

Heathcote, T.A. *The Afghan Wars: 1839-1919.* Staplehurst, Kent, UK: Spellmount Limited, 2003.

Herbst, Jeffery. *States and Power in Africa: Comparative Lessons in Authority and Control.* Princeton, NJ: Princeton University Press, 2000.

Joes, Anthony James. *Resisting Rebellion: The History and Politics of Counterinsurgency.* Lexington, KY: University of Kentucky Press, 2004.

Jullien, François. *A Treatise on Efficacy: Between Western and Chinese Thinking.* Translated by Janet Lloyd. Honolulu: University of Hawaii Press, 2004.

Kakar, M. Hassan. *Afghanistan: The Soviet Invasion and the Afghan Response, 1979-1982.* Berkeley: University of California Press, 1995.

ibn Khaldun, Abd Ar Rahman bin Muhammad. *The Muqaddimah.* 1377. Translated by Franz Rosenthal. Reprint, Princeton, NJ: Princeton University Press, 1989. http://www.muslimphilosophy.com/ik/Muqaddimah/ (accessed January 8, 2009).

McDonald, Lee Cameron. *Western Political Theory: From its Origins to the Present.* New York: Harcourt, Brace & World, 1968.

O'Neill, Bard. *Insurgency & Terrorism: From Revolution to Apocalypse.* 2nd ed. Washington, DC: Potomac Books, 2005.

Rashid, Ahmed. *Taliban: Militant Islam, Oil and Fundamentalism in Central Asia.* New Haven, CT: Yale University Press, 2000.

Riggs, Fred. *Thailand: the Modernization of a Bureaucratic Polity.* Honolulu: East-West Center Press, 1967.

Roberts, Jeffery J. *The Origins of Conflict in Afghanistan.* Westport. CT: Praeger, 2003.

Roy, Olivier. *Islam and Resistance in Afghanistan.* Cambridge, UK: Cambridge University Press, 1986. Originally published in French as *L'Afghanistan: Islam et modernité politique.* Paris: Éditions du Seuil, 1985.

Rubin, Barnett R. *The Fragmentation of Afghanistan: State Formation and the Collapse of the International System.* New Haven, CT: Yale University Press, 1995.

Saikal, Amin. *Modern Afghanistan: A History of Struggle and Survival.* New York: Tauris & Co, 2004.

Sinno, Abdulkader. "Explaining the Taliban's Ability to Mobilize the Pashtuns." In *The Taliban and the Crisis of Afghanistan.* Edited by Robert D. Crews and Amin Tarzi (Cambridge, MA: Harvard University Press, 2008), 59-89.

Tanner, Stephen. *Afghanistan: A Military History from Alexander the Great to the Fall of the Taliban.* New York: De Capo Press, 2002.

Thier, J. Alexander, ed. *The Future of Afghanistan.* Washington, DC: United States Institute of Peace, 2009.

Journal Articles, Newspaper Articles, Theses

Barfield, Thomas. "Afghan Customary Law and Its Relationship to Formal Judicial Institutions." Monograph, United States Institute for Peace, 2003.

———. "Afghanistan is Not the Balkans: Ethnicity and its Political Consequences from a Central Asian Perspective." *Central Eurasian Studies Review* 4, no, 1 (Winter 2005): 2-8.

———. "Problems in Establishing Legitimacy in Afghanistan." *Iranian Studies* 37, no. 2 (June 2004): 263-293.

CNN. "U.S., NATO Airstrikes Fuel Afghan Public Backlash," September 8, 2008. http://www.cnn.com/2008/WORLD/asiapcf/09/08/afghanistan.civilian.deaths.report/index.html (accessed March 7, 2009).

Foust, Joshua. "In Afghanistan, Good Intentions Not Enough." *World Politics Review* (March 9, 2009). http://www.worldpoliticsreview.com/article.aspx?id=3414 (accessed March 12, 2009).

Glatzer, Bernt. "War and Boundaries in Afghanistan: Significance and Relativity of Local and Social Boundaries." The Pashtun Tribal System." *Die Welt des Islams* 41, no. 3 (2001): 379-399. http://www.ag-afghanistan.de/files/war-a-bound.pdf (accessed October 2, 2008).

Human Rights Watch. "Afghanistan: Paying for the Taliban's Crimes: Abuses Against Ethnic Pashtuns in Northern Afghanistan." *Human Rights Watch* 14, no. 2 (April 2002): 1-51.

Jakes, Lara. "US Commander: Troops 'Stalemated' in Afghanistan." *Associated Press*, 18 February 2009. http://abcnews.go.com/Politics/wireStory?id=6901815 (accessed February 27, 2009).

Kakar, Palwasha. "Tribal Law of *Pashtunwali* and Women's Legislative Authority." http://www.law.harvard.edu/programs/ilsp/research/kakar.pdf (accessed September 7, 2008).

Khan, Brig. Feroz Hassan. "Rough Neighbors: Afghanistan and Pakistan." *Strategic Insights* 2, no. 2 (January 2003). http://www.ccc.nps.navy.mil/si/jan03/southAsia.asp (accessed December 15, 2008).

Noelle-Karimi, Christine."Local Perceptions of State and Law" State Reconstruction and International Engagement in Afghanistan Center for Development Research, May 30-June 1, 2003. http://www.ag-afghanistan.de/arg/arp/noelle.pdf (accessed January 8, 2009).

Robinson, Simon. "Karzai's Kabul: Fit for a King?, *Newsweek,* April 18, 2002, http://www.time.com/time/world/article/0,8599,231457,00.html (accessed March 7, 2009).

Rubin, Barnett R. "Afghan Dilemmas: Defining Commitments." *The American Interest Magazine* 3, no. 5 (May/June 2008), http://www.the-american-interest.com/ai2/article-bd.cfm?Id=423&MId=19 (accessed March 15, 2009).

————. "A Tribe Apart: Afghan Elites Face a Corrosive Past." *Boston Review,* (January/February 2009). http://bostonreview.net/BR34.1/rubin.php (accessed March 15, 2009).

Rubin, Michael. "When Pushtun Came To Shove: Who is Really Responsible for the Taliban?" *The Review* (April 2002). http://www.aijac.org.au/review/2002/274/essay274.html (accessed December 14, 2008).

Strategic Advisors Group, The Atlantic Council of the United States. "Saving Afghanistan: An Appeal and Plan for Urgent Action" (Issue Brief, March 2008). http://www.acus.org/docs/012808-AfghanistanbriefwoSAG.pdf (accessed January 27, 2009).

Wegener, Lt. Andrew. "A Complex and Changing Dynamic: Afghan Responses to Foreign Intervention, 1878-2006." Canberra, Australia: Land Warfare Studies Centre, 2007.

Radio Broadcasts, Television Broadcasts, Lectures, Remarks, Weblogs, Web Pages

The Asia Foundation. "Afghanistan in 2008: A Survey of the Afghan People." http://www.asiafoundation.org/country/afghanistan/2008-poll.php (accessed February 27, 2009).

Bleuer, Christian. "The Afghan Individual as a Unit of Analysis." The Ghosts of Alexander: The Afghan Campaign, 2001 to Whenever. Entry posted April 7, 2008. http://easterncampaign.wordpress.com/2008/04/07/the-afghan-individual-as-a-unit-of-analysis/ (accessed February 20, 2009).

————."'Afghanisation:' A Rather Unfortunate Neologism." The Ghosts of Alexander: The Afghan Campaign, 2001 to Whenever. Entry posted February 11, 2009. http://easterncampaign.wordpress.com/2009/02/11/afghanisation-a-rather-unfortunate-neologism/ (accessed April 19, 2009).

————. "Afghanistan and the *Qawm*: An Important Yet Unknown Concept." The Ghosts of Alexander: The Afghan Campaign, 2001 to Whenever. Entry posted May 6, 2007. http://easterncampaign.wordpress.com/2007/05/06/afghanistan-and-the-*qawm*-an-important-yet-unknown-concept/ (accessed February 19, 2009).

————. "Afghanistan's Local Power Structures: Exploit, Restructure, Enable or Destroy?" The Ghosts of Alexander: The Afghan Campaign, 2001 to Whenever. Entry posted March 17, 2008. http://easterncampaign.wordpress.com/2008/03/17/afghanistans-local-power-structures-exploit-restructure-or-destroy/ (accessed February 19, 2009).

————. "Pashtuns Must Have Their Revenge! Sometimes!" The Ghosts of Alexander: The Afghan Campaign, 2001 to Whenever. Entry posted June 27, 2007. http://easterncampaign.wordpress.com/2007/06/27/pashtuns-must-have-their-revenge-sometimes/ (accessed February 19, 2009).

————. "The Persistent Myth of Pre-Taliban Anarchy." The Ghosts of Alexander: The Afghan Campaign, 2001 to Whenever. Entry posted April 24, 2007. http://easterncampaign.word press.com/2007/04/24/the-persistent-myth-of-pre-taliban-anarchy/ (accessed March 15, 2009).

CIA World Factbook. "Afghanistan," https://www.cia.gov/library/publications/the-world-factbook/geos/af.html (accessed February 28, 2009).

————. "Pakistan," https://www.cia.gov/library/publications/the-world-factbook/geos/pk.html (accessed February 28, 2009).

Crocker, Ambassador Ryan. Lecture, U.S. Army Command and General Staff College, Fort Leavenworth, KS, April 23, 2009.

GlobalSecurity.org. "Operation Enduring Freedom." http://www.globalsecurity.org/military/ops/enduring-freedom-plan.htm (accessed February 27, 2009).

Exum, Andrew. "Andrew Exum on The Rachel Maddow Show." abu Muqawawa. Entry posted April 4, 2009. http://abumuqawama.blogspot.com/2009/04/andrew-exum-on-rachel-maddow.html (accessed April 6, 2009).

Foust, Joshua. "The Challenge of Tool Boxes" Registan.com. Entry posted February 18, 2009. http://www.registan.net/index.php/2009/02/18/the-challenge-of-tool-boxes/ (accessed April 29, 2009).

————. "What 'Intimate Knowledge?'" Registan.com. Entry posted September 29, 2008. http://www.registan.net/index.php/2008/09/29/quote-of-the-day-8/ (accessed April 19, 2009).

Islamic Republic of Afghanistan--Office of the President. "A Brief Biography of President Hamid Karzai." http://www.president.gov.af/english/president_biography.mspx (accessed February 27, 2009).

The Participants in the UN Talks on Afghanistan. "Agreement on Provisional Arrangements in Afghanistan Pending the Re-Establishment of Permanent Government Institutions." The United Nations. http://unama.unmissions.org/Portals/UNAMA/Documents/Bonn-agreement.pdf (accessed February 26, 2009).

Riggs, Fred. "Intellectual Odyssey: An Autobiographical Narrative First Draft," January 1999. http://www2.hawaii.edu/~fredr/autobio3.htm#3 (accessed February 20, 2009).

UN Security Council. "UN Security Council Resolution 1386 (2001) on the situation in Afghanistan." http://www.un.org/docs/scres/2001/sc2001.htm (accessed February 25, 2009).

U.S. President. Remarks. "A New Strategy for Afghanistan and Pakistan." White House Press Office. March 27, 2009. http://www.whitehouse.gov/the_press_office/Remarks-by-the-President-on-a-New-Strategy-for-Afghanistan-and-Pakistan/ (accessed May 1, 2009).

Watson, Ivan. "Experts: Lessons of Soviets in Afghanistan Ignored." *All Things Considered*, National Public Radio, June 6, 2008. http://www.npr.org/templates/story/story.php?storyId=91240615 (accessed August 28, 2008).